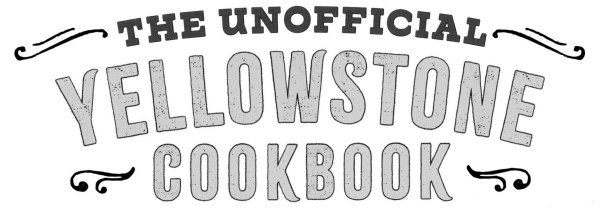

THE UNOFFICIAL YELLOWSTONE COOKBOOK

RECIPES INSPIRED BY THE DUTTON FAMILY RANCH

JACKIE ALPERS

COOK LIKE A COWBOY

From the sweeping Montana views to the honest work of the ranch hands to the inevitable conflict that comes from having to protect so much open land, *Yellowstone* represents everything that has made Westerns beloved the world over. While the series features plenty of shootouts, clapbacks and bucking broncs, it also centers around family and reinforces the importance of gathering around a dinner table to discuss the day (even if part of the day involved political scheming, revenge plotting or debating the best way to help someone plan a trip to the train station). In the following pages, we celebrate the tradition of the American Western and its modern flag-bearer, *Yellowstone*, in all their glory with recipes that the Duttons, their pioneer forebears and their staff, would be proud to enjoy while chewing the fat.

THE YELLOWSTONE KITCHEN

The Dutton kitchen reflects the bounty of their land, and their hard work. You can make yours do the same—albeit on a theoretically smaller scale.

There are plenty of reasons that folks gravitate toward *Yellowstone* when they gather around the TV, from America's historical affinity for Western fare to the intensely moving performances of the actors involved. But on a deeper level, *Yellowstone* reminds us that even in this age of DoorDash and HelloFresh, there are people out there who live a more labor-intensive—but more sustainable, rewarding and healthy—life. The Duttons might be harsh, but their ultimate goal is always the preservation of the land they love.

You should look at your pantry in the same way they look at their ranch: Is my consumption hurting the land I owe my produce to; is it a part of the wasteful industrialization folks like the Duttons have been fighting for more than a century? While you might not have a pasture full of cattle and a massive ranch on which you can hunt, fish and plant to your heart's content, following these simple tips can help you create a pantry that's more self-sustaining, less wasteful and much, much more traditionally Western.

SAY TA-TA TO YOUR TEFLON

ONE SIMPLE WAY you can emulate old-timey Western kitchen philosophy is to invest in long-lasting, heavy-duty cookware. Teflon-lined pans might be convenient in the short term, but they ultimately create more waste (because they only last a year or two in good condition, whereas a well-made piece of cookware can become an heirloom) and offer less flavor thanks to the chemicals in the lining, which make it impossible for the flavors and character of, for example, a good cast iron pan, to develop over time.

GROW SOMETHING

WHETHER YOU HAVE a few acres, a small front garden or a flower box by the window, grow something—anything—that you can incorporate into your pantry. Herbs like basil or rosemary are popular for small-scale dabbling, as are tomatoes and peppers for mid-sized plots. Plus, there's nothing like the feeling of saving yourself a trip to the store because you grew your produce yourself.

SAVE YOUR SCRAPS

IF YOU CAN save your organic kitchen scraps and have the space to compost them, the resulting soil will be rich in nutrients and yield even better produce from whatever plot of land you're cultivating, whether it's a window box or a full acre.

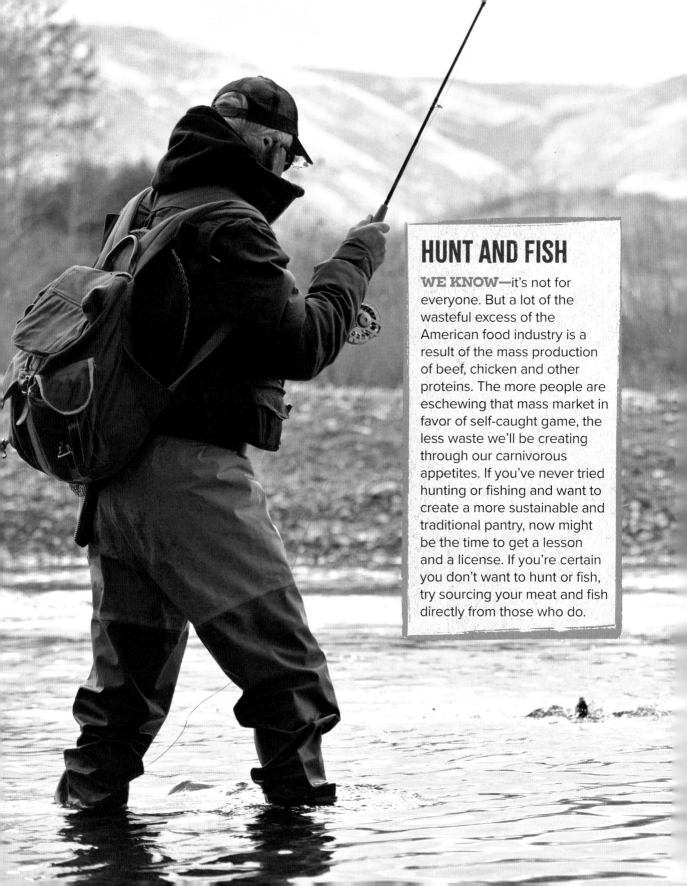

HUNT AND FISH

WE KNOW—it's not for everyone. But a lot of the wasteful excess of the American food industry is a result of the mass production of beef, chicken and other proteins. The more people are eschewing that mass market in favor of self-caught game, the less waste we'll be creating through our carnivorous appetites. If you've never tried hunting or fishing and want to create a more sustainable and traditional pantry, now might be the time to get a lesson and a license. If you're certain you don't want to hunt or fish, try sourcing your meat and fish directly from those who do.

SHOP SMART

WHEN YOU GO shopping, do so with a mind toward the source: Was this produce locally grown? Is it fresh, or has it come from across the continent in the back of a series of trains and trucks? Were these chickens free-range or from a factory farm? Was this fish pole-caught, farmed or caught in a dangerous and wasteful industrial net? The answers to these questions not only mean the difference between a good dinner and a great one—they can also make a huge difference in terms of your environmental impact.

JAR, CAN AND DRY

ANY SURPLUS PRODUCE or meat should be preserved by canning, pickling, dehydrating or whatever other traditional methods you choose. A big part of the cowboy diet has always been easy-to-carry fare such as dried fruits, jerky and preserves, and as a wise man said, "Waste not, want not."

Wild horses stampede in Montana. Many of the horses used on *Yellowstone* belong to series creator Taylor Sheridan.

Johnny (Dutton) Cakes, pg. 34.

BREAKFAST

There won't be any need to yell
"Up and at 'em": The delicious smells alone
will rouse any bunkhouse in the West
(or wherever you hail from) as if Gator
himself were manning the skillet.

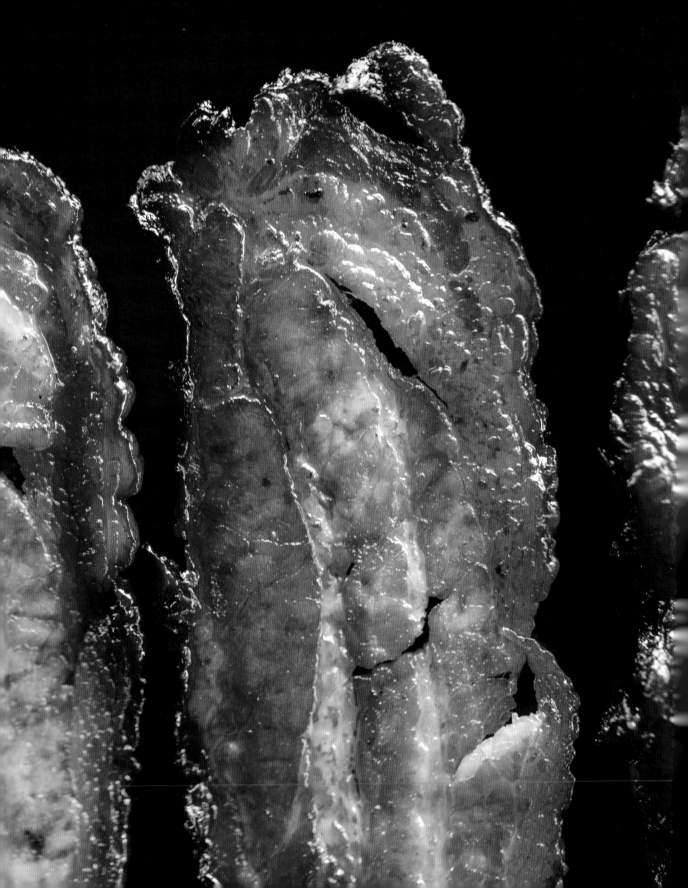

Up and at 'Em Hot Honey Bacon

YELLOWSTONE MIGHT BE IN THE HEART OF CATTLE COUNTRY, BUT THERE'S NO DENYING THE APPEAL OF A HEAP OF SMOKY BACON BEFORE A DAY OF HARD WORK OR HIGH INTRIGUE.

PREP TIME 5 MINUTES
COOK TIME 10–12 MINUTES
YIELD 8–10 SLICES

INGREDIENTS

- ¼ cup red wine vinegar
- ½ cup hot honey, such as Mike's Hot Honey
- 1 lb slab bacon, sliced ⅛–¼ inch thick

DIRECTIONS

1. Preheat the oven to 375 degrees F.
2. Line a baking sheet with foil, then set an oven-safe wire rack on top.
3. Whisk vinegar into honey until well combined.
4. Lay each strip of bacon flat on the rack, brush top with the honey mixture, then flip and brush the other side.
5. Bake for 10 to 12 minutes or until desired crispness is achieved.

COWBOY COFFEE

All cowboys know that eggshells make coffee cooked over the high heat of a campfire less acidic.

INGREDIENTS

- 1 quart water
- 4–6 eggshells
- 1 cup of ground coffee

DIRECTIONS

Bring the water to a boil in a fire-safe coffee pot. Break the eggshells into pieces and mix in with the ground coffee. Remove the pot from the heat and add the coffee and eggshells. Let steep for 5 minutes, then pour into mugs, careful to not disturb the grounds and eggshells at the bottom of the pot.

Texas Cowboy Breakfast Tacos

THIS RECIPE CALLS FOR TWO TORTILLAS PER TACO TO HOLD THE EXTRA HEFT OF TACOS THE SIZE OF TEXAS, WHERE JIMMY MOVES TO LIVE OUT HIS LARGER-THAN-LIFE RODEO DREAMS.

PREP TIME 20 MINUTES
COOK TIME 5 MINUTES
YIELD 4 TACOS

INGREDIENTS

- 8 (6-inch) high-quality flour or corn tortillas
- 4 roasted Hatch or Anaheim chiles
- 4 strips prepared bacon, see pg. 13
- 4 eggs, fried in butter until edges are crispy and yolks are set
- 1 cup shredded sharp cheddar cheese
- Salsa or hot sauce to taste

DIRECTIONS

1. Heat a skillet over medium heat and warm the tortillas for a minute or 2 on each side.
2. Put 2 tortillas on a plate so they overlap halfway in the middle. Lay a roasted chile down the middle, tuck in a slice of bacon, then saddle with the fried egg.
3. Top with cheese and salsa, fold and enjoy.

TIPS FROM THE TRAIL

Use the best quality tortillas you can find. Look for ones that are not too white or too fluffy.

Oatmeal Bowls With Maple Brown Butter Apples

WHETHER YOU'RE SITTING AROUND A CAMPFIRE BEFORE A LONG CATTLE DRIVE OR GEARING UP TO ORCHESTRATE THE FINANCIAL SLAUGHTER OF A RIVAL COMPANY, THIS OATMEAL IS SIMPLE ENOUGH TO GET YOU READY FOR A DAY'S WORK WITH EASE.

PREP TIME 10–20 MINUTES
COOK TIME 10 MINUTES
YIELD 4 SERVINGS

INGREDIENTS

- 2 Honeycrisp or Granny Smith apples
- 1 lemon, juiced
- ½ cup butter, preferably grass-fed
- ½ cup pure maple syrup, plus more for serving
- 1 Tbsp chia seeds
- 1 tsp vanilla
- 4 cups prepared oatmeal
- ½ cup dried sour cherries
- ½ cup dried blueberries
- 1 tsp cinnamon, divided
- ½ tsp cane sugar, divided
- Milk or cream for serving, optional

DIRECTIONS

1. Cut the apples widthwise into thin slices, then sprinkle the lemon juice over both sides of the apple slices to prevent browning.

2. Heat the butter and maple syrup in a large, deep nonstick skillet over medium heat until gently bubbling. Carefully lay a single layer of apple slices in the pan, in batches, and cook for a minute on each side. Set aside, reserving remaining maple brown butter sauce for serving.

3. Stir the chia seeds and vanilla into the prepared oatmeal. Divide into 4 bowls. Arrange the apples, cherries and blueberries on top. Spoon maple brown butter sauce on top. Sprinkle each bowl with ¼ tsp of cinnamon and ⅛ tsp of cane sugar and serve with maple syrup and milk or cream.

Bigger Than Texas Breakfast Sandwich

PAN AZTECA MAKES THESE TEX-MEX SANDWICHES UNIQUELY DELICIOUS. AFTER ONE BITE YOU'LL REALIZE WHY JIMMY HURDSTROM ISN'T THE ONLY ONE WHO ASSOCIATES TEXAS WITH THE COWBOY LIFE.

PREP TIME 15 MINUTES
COOK TIME 30 MINUTES
YIELD 4 SANDWICHES

INGREDIENTS

- 4   pan azteca or bolillo rolls, halved
- 2   cups refried beans, warmed
- 1   cup white Mexican cheese, such as queso fresco
- ½   cup ranch dressing
- 1   Tbsp adobo sauce from a jar of chipotle peppers in adobo
- 8   sausage patties, warmed
- 4   roasted Hatch or Anaheim chiles
- 1   avocado, peeled and roughly chopped
- 4   thick slices red onion
- 8   strips prepared bacon, see pg. 13
- 4   eggs, fried until the edges are crispy
   Hot sauce, for serving

DIRECTIONS

1. Slather both sides of a pan azteca roll with beans, then top with a generous portion of cheese and toast until the cheese is melted and starting to brown.

2. While the bread is toasting, mix the ranch dressing and adobo sauce in a small bowl.

3. Lay 2 sausage patties on the bottom half of the roll, then spread on the sauce and top with a roasted chile, ¼ of the chopped avocado, 1 onion slice, 2 strips of bacon and a fried egg. Balance the other half of the roll on top of your sandwich and serve with hot sauce—and plenty of napkins.

TIPS FROM THE TRAIL

If you can't find pan azteca locally, look for a similar sturdy, crusty roll with some heft to it. Bolillo rolls are similar to demi baguettes, which also work well for this.

Fry Bread With Thick-Cut Bacon and Scrambled Ranch Eggs

ON *YELLOWSTONE*, RIP PREPARES FRY BREAD AS A BREAKFAST FOR TWO AFTER SPENDING THE NIGHT WITH BETH, PROVING EVEN THE TOUGHEST COWBOY CAN HAVE A FEW CULINARY TRICKS UP HIS SLEEVE.

PREP TIME 15 MINUTES
COOK TIME 30 MINUTES
YIELD 6–8 SERVINGS

INGREDIENTS

- 1 cup all-purpose flour, plus more for your hands
- 1 tsp baking powder
- 1 tsp powdered milk or powdered buttermilk
- ¼ tsp sea salt
- ½ cup water
- Neutral-flavored cooking oil, such as canola, for frying

DIRECTIONS

1. Whisk together dry ingredients in mixing bowl. Add the water and stir with a fork until crumbly, clumpy and well combined. Knead briefly (about 10 times) with your hands. (Over-kneading will make the fry bread less fluffy.) Form into a ball. The dough will be somewhat sticky so you will need to keep your hands well-floured.

2. Heat an inch of cooking oil in a large Dutch oven to 350 degrees F. Use a cooking thermometer to keep temperature consistent.

3. Portion the dough into 6 to 8 even pieces and flatten with your hands to a half inch thick by 6 to 8 inches across.

4. Gently place a piece of flattened dough into the oil and cook for 1 to 2 minutes on each side, flipping with tongs. Drain on paper towels.

5. Top each piece with 2 scrambled eggs and 2 pieces of prepared bacon.

A NOTE ON FRY BREAD

The fact that Rip's go-to recipe is fry bread speaks to the constant blending of cultures highlighted on *Yellowstone*, illustrating what makes the West so special. Like many of the world's exceedingly delicious dishes, fry bread was born out of poverty and necessity. When the U.S. relocated the Navajo Nation in their campaign to conquer the continent from sea to sea, the refugees were given simple canned foods, lard, flour and sugar—all staples for their long, difficult journey. The latter three ingredients soon became the first fry bread, and the delicious yet simple fare has been ubiquitous in many native cuisines ever since.

TIPS FROM THE TRAIL

Rip makes his fry bread in a cast-iron skillet, but because boiling oil is involved, it's safer to make yours in a large Dutch oven.

Parmesan and Chive Scones

WHEN *YELLOWSTONE* LEAVES THE RANCH AND HEADS TO THE CITY, GOVERNMENTAL AND BUSINESS MEETINGS FEATURE POSH SPREADS OF TASTY GOODIES LIKE THESE SAVORY SCONES.

PREP TIME 20 MINUTES
COOK TIME 20–25 MINUTES
YIELD 8 SCONES

INGREDIENTS

- 1½ tsp kosher salt
- 1 tsp black pepper
- 2 tsp baking powder
- ½ tsp baking soda
- 1 tsp sugar
- 2½ cups all-purpose flour, plus more for surface prep
- 10 Tbsp chilled unsalted butter, cut into ½-inch pieces
- 1 cup shredded Parmesan cheese, divided
- ½ oz chives (about 1 package), roughly chopped, divided
- 1 egg, lightly beaten
- 1¼ cups plain Greek yogurt

DIRECTIONS

1. Preheat the oven to 425 degrees F. Line 2 baking sheets with parchment or baking mats.
2. Whisk the salt, pepper, baking powder, baking soda, sugar and flour in a large bowl. Toss butter pieces in flour mixture to coat, then, using your fingers, break apart the butter with a snapping motion until you have lots of small chips of coated butter.
3. Fold in ½ cup Parmesan and ¼ cup chives.
4. Create a well in the middle of the mixture. Spoon the egg and yogurt into the middle and stir with a fork until large clumps form.
5. Turn the dough out onto a floured surface and pat and form into a 1-inch-thick rectangle. Fold into thirds, like you would fold a letter, then repeat the patting and folding process.
6. Cut the rectangle in half so that you have 2 squares, then cut diagonally in an X making a total of 8 triangles of dough. Arrange on a baking sheet at least ½ inch apart. Sprinkle the reserved chives then the reserved Parmesan on top.
7. Bake for 20 to 25 minutes or until bottoms are golden brown. Let cool slightly before serving.

Tate's Choice Glazed Doughnuts

THE YOUNGEST DUTTON IS CERTAINLY NOT ALONE WHEN IT COMES TO HIS LOVE OF DOUGHNUTS, AND ONCE YOU TASTE THESE, YOU'LL START ASKING FOR THEM BY NAME.

PREP TIME 1 HOUR
WAIT TIME 3 HOURS
COOK TIME 30–45 MINUTES
YIELD 10–12 DOUGHNUTS AND 12 DOUGHNUT HOLES

INGREDIENTS

- 2 cups all-purpose flour
- ¼ cup granulated sugar
- ½ tsp ground cinnamon
- ¼ tsp salt
- ¼ cup milk, warmed to about **100 degrees F**
- ¼ cup water, warmed to about **100 degrees F**
- 2¼ tsp (1 packet) instant dry yeast
- 1 egg
- 3 Tbsp unsalted butter, melted and cooled
  About 3 cups oil, such as canola, for frying

GLAZE

- 1½ cups confectioners' sugar
- ½ tsp pure vanilla extract
- ⅛ tsp salt
- 2–3 Tbsp milk

DIRECTIONS

1. In a large mixing bowl, combine the flour, sugar, cinnamon and salt.

2. In another mixing bowl, whisk together milk and water, sprinkle in the yeast, then stir in the egg and melted butter.

3. Make a well in the middle of the dry ingredients, pour in the wet ingredients and stir with a rubber spatula to combine.

4. For 10 to 15 minutes, knead dough on a work surface greased with a bit of cooking oil or use an electric stand mixer fitted with a dough hook. The dough will start out very sticky but will be firmer when ready to rise.

5. Scrape down the sides of the bowl if using an electric mixer. If kneading by hand, put the dough in a lightly oiled bowl. Cover and let stand for 2 hours or until doubled.

6. Roll out dough on a floured surface to about ½-inch thick. Using a doughnut cutter or 2 circular cookie cutters (1 small, 1 large), cut out doughnuts and place on parchment- or baking mat-lined baking sheets. Roll scraps into 1-to-2-inch doughnut holes.

7. Cover and let rise for another hour.

8. Heat an inch of cooking oil in a large Dutch oven to 330 degrees F. Use a cooking thermometer to keep temperature consistent.

9. Gently lower doughnuts into the hot oil in batches of 2 or 3 to keep them from colliding; turn them over as they rise to the surface. Fry until golden brown, about 1 to 2 minutes per side.

10. Transfer doughnuts to a wire rack on a baking sheet to drain and cool.

11. To prepare the glaze, whisk together sugar, vanilla extract and salt. Add 2 tablespoons milk and whisk to blend, adding the additional tablespoon as needed to create a shiny, pourable glaze.

12. Spoon glaze over cooled doughnuts. Let glaze set for about 10 minutes before serving.

Choco Chimps Cereal Treat

AFTER GATOR SLAVES AWAY TO CREATE A PERFECT HOT BREAKFAST FOR JOHN AND TATE, THEY DECIDE THEY'D RATHER HAVE A HEAPING BOWL OF CHOCO CHIMPS, TATE'S FAVORITE CEREAL. TURNS OUT, CHOCO CHIMPS ARE REAL, AND WE TURNED THEM INTO A NEW CHEWY TREAT!

PREP TIME 2 HOURS, 20 MINUTES
YIELD 8–10 SERVINGS

INGREDIENTS

Butter cooking spray

⅓ cup pure maple syrup, room temperature, plus more as needed

1 cup smooth or chunky peanut or other nut butter, room temperature

1 Tbsp butter, melted

1 tsp vanilla extract

1 box (approximately 6 cups) Choco Chimps cereal (or organic cocoa-flavored cereal of your choice)

1 cup dehydrated, sliced strawberries

Sprinkles, optional

DIRECTIONS

1. Grease an 8-inch star-shaped mold or 8-by-8-inch baking pan with butter cooking spray. Set aside.

2. In a 2 cup or larger mixing cup or medium, high-sided bowl, add the maple syrup, peanut butter, melted butter and vanilla extract; stir with a butter knife until well combined.

3. Pour the cereal into a large mixing bowl. With a rubber spatula, gently fold in the maple syrup mixture to coat. Be careful to not squash the cereal. If the mixture is not holding together, add an additional tablespoon of maple syrup, then carefully fold in the strawberries.

4. Press the cereal mixture into a mold or baking pan. Cover with wax paper and press to fill, adding more of the mixture in any open pockets. Top with sprinkles. Refrigerate for at least 2 hours. Flip onto a flat surface to remove from the mold. Cut and serve.

TIPS FROM THE TRAIL

This recipe eschews marshmallows, the traditional binding agent in crispy treats like these, but if you're not counting calories, you're welcome to reintroduce marshmallows to the party.

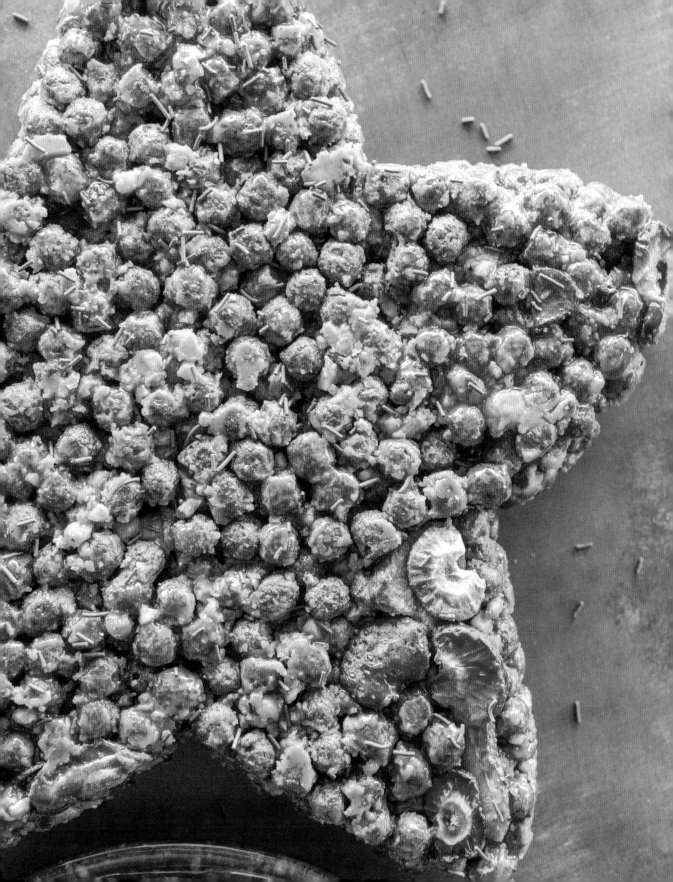

Big Sky Country Cinnamon Roll

THE ONLY THING MORE IMPRESSIVE THAN THESE TREATS FIT FOR A CATTLE BARON IS BEING ABLE TO FINISH ONE OFF IN A SINGLE SITTING.

PREP TIME 10 MINUTES
COOK TIME 20–25 MINUTES
YIELD 6–8 SERVINGS

INGREDIENTS

- Butter cooking spray
- 1 can refrigerated cinnamon roll dough with glaze
- 1 Tbsp huckleberry or blueberry preserves

TIPS FROM THE TRAIL

To keep things simple, we used refrigerated cinnamon roll dough for this recipe, but feel free to make it from scratch!

DIRECTIONS

1. Preheat the oven to 350 degrees F. Spray an 8- or 9-inch cast-iron skillet with butter cooking spray. Separate the dough into 5 rolls. Set the glaze aside.

2. Place 1 roll face up in the center of the cast-iron skillet. Carefully unroll one of the other rolls into 1 long strip. Find the endpoint of the dough on the outside of the roll sitting in the skillet and connect one end of the unraveled strip to it. Then spiral the dough around the roll filling side on the inside. Continue the process with the other 3 rolls until you have 1 giant cinnamon roll. If some of the cinnamon falls off in the process, tuck it back into any empty nooks and crannies.

3. Bake for 20 to 25 minutes or until golden brown. Let cool for 5 minutes.

4. While the cinnamon roll is cooling, microwave the glaze at 50 percent power for 15 seconds.

5. Spoon 2 tablespoons of the glaze into a separate bowl and stir in preserves to combine.

6. Brush the berry glaze over the cinnamon roll with a pastry brush so that it is thicker in areas, then brush the remaining parts of the cinnamon roll with the remaining glaze as shown.

7. Cut into wedges and serve warm.

Cornmeal Mush

THOSE SEEKING OPPORTUNITY ACROSS THE WESTERN TRAILS, LIKE THE FOLKS ON *1883*, HAD TO SUPPLEMENT WHAT THEY COULD CATCH ALONG THE WAY WITH EASY-TO-STORE IMPERISHABLES. THIS CORNMEAL PORRIDGE WOULD HAVE BEEN A COMMON SUPPLEMENT TO WILD GAME FOR A FAST AND EASY MEAL.

PREP TIME 5 MINUTES
COOK TIME 10 MINUTES
YIELD 4 SERVINGS

INGREDIENTS

- 2 cups water, divided
- ½ cup cornmeal
- ½ tsp sea salt
- Butter and syrup, for serving

DIRECTIONS

1. Boil 1½ cups water in a medium saucepan.

2. Combine cornmeal and salt with ½ cup water in a small bowl or measuring cup. Slowly pour the cornmeal mixture into the boiling water while stirring constantly. Cook 1 to 2 minutes or until thickened and most of the water is absorbed.

3. Remove from heat, cover and let sit for 5 minutes. Stir and serve with butter and syrup or let cool and form into corn cakes (see pg. 32).

Corn Cakes

WHEN GATHERING AROUND THE CAMPFIRE TO COOK, A SIMPLE CORNMEAL MUSH LIKE THE ONE ON THE PREVIOUS SPREAD CAN BECOME A CLASSIC NATIVE AMERICAN DISH, AS SEEN ON *YELLOWSTONE*.

PREP TIME 20 MINUTES
COOK TIME 30 MINUTES
YIELD 6–8 CORN CAKES

INGREDIENTS

2 cups cornmeal mush (see pg. 30), cooled
1 Tbsp butter, more if needed
1 Tbsp vegetable or nut oil, more if needed

DIRECTIONS

1. Wet your hands, grab a portion of cornmeal mush and form into a patty about ½-inch thick by 3 to 4 inches across. Heat the butter and oil in a large skillet over medium heat.
2. Fry 2 to 3 corn cakes at a time until browned, about 3 to 4 minutes per side, adding more oil and butter if needed to prevent sticking. Do not overcrowd. Transfer to a baking sheet and keep in a warm oven until ready to serve.

BETH'S RESTORATIVE SMOOTHIE

The perfect addition to this breakfast? A hearty smoothie to help you recover from a long night of vodka and olives (pg. 90) or an attempted murder.

INGREDIENTS

2 scoops Baskin-Robbins Triple Mango ice cream
3 shots (4½ oz) vodka
Orange slice, for garnish
Maraschino cherry, for garnish

DIRECTIONS

Put ice cream and vodka in a high-speed blender and blitz until well combined. Fling the orange slice and Maraschino cherry into the bushes then drink through a straw.

Johnny (Dutton) Cakes

A FANCIER ALTERNATIVE TO SIMPLE CORN CAKES, THESE ARE TAKEN UP A LEVEL BY FRESH OR DRIED BERRIES.

PREP TIME 10 MINUTES
WAIT TIME 5 MINUTES
COOK TIME 15 MINUTES
YIELD 8–10 JOHNNY CAKES

INGREDIENTS

- 1 cup all-purpose flour
- 1 cup coarsely ground cornmeal
- 1 Tbsp baking powder
- ¼ tsp kosher salt
- 2 eggs, lightly beaten
- 1 cup buttermilk
- ¼ cup water
- 2 Tbsp butter, plus more for serving
  Pure maple syrup, for serving
- 2 cups fresh or dried blueberries or huckleberries, for serving

DIRECTIONS

1. Whisk together the flour, cornmeal, baking powder and salt in a large mixing bowl.
2. Stir in the eggs, buttermilk and water and mix with a rubber spatula until well combined. The batter will be very thick. Let it sit for 5 to 10 minutes while you heat up a large nonstick skillet and melt the butter over medium heat.
3. Ladle about ½ cup of batter into the pan in batches, being careful not to crowd and giving yourself room to flip easily. Cook for 3 to 5 minutes on each side. They won't bubble the way pancakes do, so you'll need to make sure they're brown enough on the bottom first.
4. Lay in a single layer on a parchment- or baking mat-lined baking sheet and keep in a warm oven until ready to serve.
5. Stack the cakes, top with a pat of butter, pour on the syrup and toss on some berries.

TIPS FROM THE TRAIL

We used blueberries to top these cakes, but you're welcome to experiment with your favorite combinations of berries, stone fruit and more.

Bunkhouse Breakfast

BEFORE A BIG DAY LIKE A CATTLE AUCTION OR RODEO, THE FOLKS IN THE BUNKHOUSE NEED AS MUCH FUEL AS THEY CAN GET. THIS SAVORY STEAK AND MUSHROOM SKILLET DOES THE TRICK.

PREP TIME 30 MINUTES

COOK TIME 10 MINUTES

YIELD 2 SERVINGS

INGREDIENTS

- 1 Tbsp butter
- 4 eggs
  Sea salt
  Freshly ground black pepper
- 2 thinly cut (about ⅛-to-¼-inch thick) breakfast steaks, room temperature
  Cast Iron Roasted Mushrooms (recipe below)
  Brown gravy, see pg. 167
  Dried or fresh oregano, for serving

DIRECTIONS

1. Melt the butter in a cast-iron skillet over medium-low heat. Gently crack in the eggs, season with salt and pepper and cook until the edges are crispy, whites are white and yolks are set, about 5 to 8 minutes. It will take longer to cook the eggs than the steaks.

2. Season one side of the steaks with sea salt and a generous grind of black pepper. Then flip the steaks onto a griddle on medium-high before seasoning the other side. Cook for a minute or 2 or until the steaks release their juices, then flip and cook for a minute or 2 more.

3. Spoon the mushrooms onto the plates, then layer on the steak and eggs, pour on the gravy and garnish with oregano.

CAST IRON ROASTED MUSHROOMS

PREP TIME 5 MINUTES

COOK TIME 25–30 MINUTES

YIELD MAKES 2–4 SERVINGS

INGREDIENTS

- 1 (8-oz) container sliced mushrooms, any variety
  Olive oil spray
  Salt and pepper to taste
- ¼ cup diced red onion or shallots
- 1 Tbsp red wine vinegar

DIRECTIONS

1. Preheat the oven to 350 degrees F.

2. Put the mushrooms in a cast iron skillet. Spray lightly with olive oil and season with salt and pepper.

3. Roast for 25 to 30 minutes, stirring occasionally, until they are soft and darkened.

4. Remove from the oven and toss with red wine vinegar.

Gator's Crispy Montana-Style Hash Browns

DON'T BE PUT OFF BY THE HEFTY INGREDIENTS LIST: THESE HASH BROWNS ARE BOTH SIMPLE TO MAKE AND THE PERFECT ADDITION TO ALMOST ANY BREAKFAST. THE DUTTON FAMILY CHEF WOULD BE WISE TO KEEP THIS ONE IN MIND.

PREP TIME 15 MINUTES

COOK TIME 15 MINUTES

YIELD 8 SERVINGS

INGREDIENTS

- 4 cups shredded potatoes (pre-shredded potatoes are best)
- ½ cup diced red onion
- ½ cup diced Poblano or Anaheim chiles
- ½ tsp oregano
- ½ tsp thyme
- ½ tsp rosemary
- ½ tsp smoked paprika
- ½ tsp sea salt
- ¼ tsp black pepper
- ½ cup shredded sharp cheddar, plus more for sprinkling
- 1 cup salsa, for serving

DIRECTIONS

1. Microwave the shredded potatoes, onions and chiles together for 4 minutes. Let cool slightly then stir in herbs and cheese. Flatten ½ cup of the mixture between 2 pieces of parchment paper to ¼ inch thick.

2. Flip onto a lightly greased nonstick skillet and sprinkle evenly with cheese.

3. Cook over medium heat for 4 to 5 minutes. Lay a large griddle press, silicone baking mat or lipless pan lid on top. Flip the skillet so that the hash brown is laying on the griddle press, then gently slide the hash browns back into the pan. Sprinkle the exposed side with more cheese and cook for an additional 4 to 5 minutes. Slide the hash brown onto a plate. Repeat to use all the mixture. Serve with salsa.

TIPS FROM THE TRAIL

If you want to make crispy hash browns with less mess, use an air fryer. Give the hash browns a light coating of oil before tossing them into the basket.

TIPS FROM THE TRAIL

A Western staple, elk sausage is best cooked low and slow. Aim for an internal temperature of 130 degrees F but not over 140. It's okay if the sausage is a little bit pink inside.

Flathead Forest Elk Sausage Patties

WHEN UNWELCOME ANIMAL GUESTS SHOW UP ON A RANCH LIKE THE YELLOWSTONE, IT'S NOT UNCOMMON FOR SOME OF THE RESULTING MEAT TO SHOW UP IN THE BUNKHOUSE KITCHEN: THESE ELK SAUSAGES ARE THE PERFECT REPRESENTATION OF HOW PROPER HANDS MAKE THE MOST OF WHAT THEY GET.

PREP TIME 10 MINUTES
WAIT TIME 1 HOUR
COOK TIME 20–30 MINUTES
YIELD 8–10 SAUSAGE PATTIES

INGREDIENTS

- 1 lb ground elk
- 1 tsp hot sauce
- 1 Tbsp pure maple syrup
- 1 Tbsp fennel seeds
- 1 Tbsp onion flakes
- 2 Tbsp chopped fresh sage leaves
- 1 tsp smoked paprika, hot or mild
- 1 tsp dried oregano
- 1 tsp granulated garlic
- 1 tsp course sea salt
- ½ tsp fresh or dried thyme
- ¼ tsp ground black pepper

DIRECTIONS

1. Put the ground elk in a large mixing bowl and mix in the rest of the ingredients with your hands or a rubber spatula until well combined. Cover and refrigerate for at least an hour to let the flavors meld.

2. Roll into 2-oz balls, then flatten with wet hands until each patty is about ½ inch thick by 2 inches across.

3. Cook in a large nonstick skillet over medium-low heat for 3 to 6 minutes on each side, pressing down with a spatula for a few seconds to flatten patties.

WILD GAME

For the many Americans who enjoy bringing home their own meat by hunting, one of the most satisfying parts of the ritual is stocking the freezer with enough meat to feed your family for the winter, no grocery store required. We used elk for these sausage patties, but depending on where you are and what season it is, elk might not be possible to put on the table. The good news is we've used universal flavors that will work with venison, wild boar or whatever red meat you're able to bag.

Biscuits and Sausage Gravy

TATE MIGHT PREFER HIS CHOCOLATE CEREAL, BUT WHEN GATOR GETS GOING WITH HIS TRADITIONAL COMFORT FARE, LIKE THESE BISCUITS, WE CAN'T IMAGINE ANYTHING BETTER.

PREP TIME 5 MINUTES
COOK TIME 10 MINUTES
YIELD 4 SERVINGS

INGREDIENTS

- 8 biscuits, halved, see pg. 165
- 4 cups sausage gravy, see pg. 161
  Smoked paprika, for serving
  Dried oregano, for serving

DIRECTIONS

1. Lay a halved biscuit on a large plate, cut side up. Ladle on plenty of gravy over each half, then sprinkle with paprika and toss on some dried oregano so you can say you've eaten your greens.

2. Top with a couple of poached, scrambled or fried eggs if you're hankering for more protein.

Paradise Valley in the Gallatin National Forest north of Yellowstone National Park. Although the show takes place in Montana, most of the national park is located in Wyoming.

Maple Bacon Popcorn,
pg. 64.

STARTERS & SNACKS

Whether you need to whip up some serious hors d'oeuvres or just want a little something between meals, you can keep the big house or the bunkhouse happy with these recipes.

Saddle Pack Jerky

WHEN YOU SPEND A LONG DAY DRIVING CATTLE (OR JUST DRIVING TO THE OFFICE), YOU CAN WORK UP AN APPETITE. KEEP YOUR STOMACH FROM GROWLING WITH THIS OLD MAINSTAY.

PREP TIME 10 MINUTES
COOK TIME 6–8 HOURS
YIELD 4–6 SERVINGS

INGREDIENTS

- 2   lb steak, thinly cut
- 2   Tbsp red pepper flakes, optional
     Sea salt

DIRECTIONS

1. Preheat oven or food dehydrator to 170 degrees F.
2. Pound the steak with the pyramid-textured side of a heavy meat mallet to approximately ⅛ inch thick. Season both sides with red pepper flakes and sea salt.
3. Transfer to a baking sheet lined with an oven-safe rack and dry until brittle, about 6 to 8 hours, depending on meat thickness.

CENTURIES OF SNACKING

Jerky has been a staple snack in South America since long before Europeans ever arrived, but the first written evidence we have dates from the Spanish conquest of the Quechua tribe in the 1500s. In that tribe's language, the preparation of beef that would become a staple of road trips and campfires was known as ch'arki: "to burn (meat)." Of course, when the Spanish made their way into North America, they found more and more tribes who were preserving their meat in the same way—but it was the Quechua word that stuck.

TIPS FROM THE TRAIL

This recipe uses beef, but you can also use other thinly sliced meat, such as bison or elk, for an especially Western experience. Once dried, the jerky can be stored in an airtight container for one to two months.

Pan-Charred Peanuts in the Shell

IF THERE'S A MORE CLASSIC SNACK TO ENJOY WHILE KICKING BACK IN THE BUNKHOUSE AFTER A HARD DAY, WE COULDN'T NAME IT.

PREP TIME 14–18 HOURS
COOK TIME 30–40 MINUTES
YIELD 4–6 SERVINGS

INGREDIENTS

- ½ cup kosher salt
- 1 quart warm water
- 1 lb raw in-shell peanuts, washed

DIRECTIONS

1. Dissolve salt in warm water. Pour in the peanuts and soak for 6 hours to infuse.

2. Discard the water, then let the peanuts dry for 8 to 12 hours or overnight. The peanuts must be fully dry before cooking.

3. Preheat oven to 350 degrees F. In large cast iron pans, arrange the peanuts in a single layer so they are all in direct contact with the surface. Roast 30 to 40 minutes, stirring occasionally until the shells are charred as shown.

4. Test for doneness by removing a peanut from its shell. It should be very hot to the touch. Let cool and serve.

RETURN TO SOUTH AMERICA

Peanuts, like beef jerky, were enjoyed by native South American cultures for centuries before being "discovered" by Europeans. Finding the native legume tasty and versatile, Spanish conquistadors brought it back to Europe, where traders in turn took it around the world. It might now feature in cuisines as diverse as Ethiopian, Thai and Indonesian, but they all trace their roots to these simple snacks.

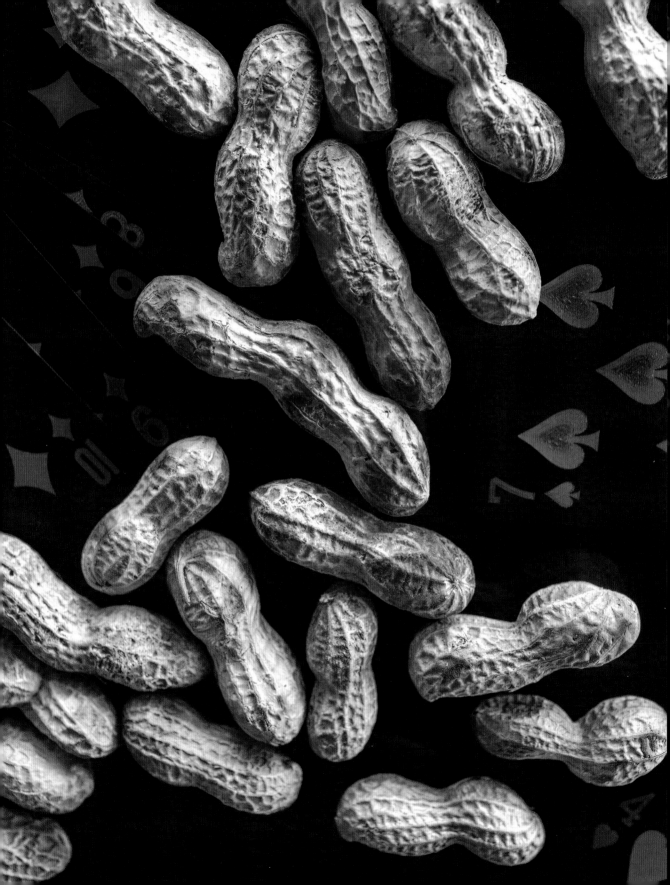

Sheepherders' Hors d'Oeuvres

THESE SNACKS ARE A BEACON OF FAMILIAR FLAVORS HAILING FROM THE DUTTONS' VERY BACKYARD. THE SIMPLE COMBO OF ONION, ORANGE AND CHEESE IS A SWEET AND SALTY DELIGHT. DON'T KNOCK IT 'TIL YOU'VE TRIED IT.

PREP TIME 15 MINUTES

YIELD 4 SERVINGS

INGREDIENTS

- 1 sleeve of saltines, about 40
- 6 oz cheddar cheese, sliced into saltine-sized squares
- 3–4 small oranges, such as clementines or mandarins, sectioned
- 1 small white onion, thinly sliced

DIRECTIONS

Arrange the saltines on a platter. Layer cheddar, orange sections and onion slices on top.

A MONTANA TRADITION

According to the *Great Falls Tribune*, these off-beat apps are a staple at Jersey Lilly Bar and Cafe in Ingomar, Montana (population: 14). The town was once a center for sheep shearing and wool trading, and the name of these hors d'oeuvres is a throwback to this bygone trade. Exactly who thought of this unique combination of flavors has been lost to time, but the dish remains a staple at Jersey Lilly.

TIPS FROM THE TRAIL

While these starters are most often prepared in the traditional manner, you can experiment with different flavor crackers and different sharp cheeses.

Wild West Meat and Cheese Board

IN SEASON 2, TATE GOES ON HIS FIRST HUNTING TRIP, A POWERFUL MOMENT FOR THREE GENERATIONS OF DUTTON MEN. YOU DON'T HAVE TO BAG YOUR OWN WILD GAME TO MAKE THIS APP TRAY, BUT IF YOU'RE BURSTING WITH COWBOY SPIRIT, YOU'RE WELCOME TO!

PREP TIME 30 MINUTES

YIELD 4–6 SERVINGS

INGREDIENTS

- Marcona almonds with rosemary
- Barrio Bread's pain au levain, sliced and quartered
- Fig and olive crackers
- Sliced lomo dry-cured pork loin
- Rutland Red cheese
- Wild boar salami from feral Texas swine
- Sliced duck prosciutto
- White truffle butter, room temperature
- Sliced Lonzino dry-cured pork loin
- Dry-cured duck breast
- More crackers, bread and almonds to surround

DIRECTIONS

Place a large dollop of the truffle butter directly on the board then arrange the thinly sliced meats artfully on the board with remaining ingredients.

TIPS FROM THE TRAIL

Angel's Salumi & Truffles provided the cured meats and truffle butter shown here. They ship nationwide, making it easy to expand your culinary horizons with unexpected proteins. For very thin slices, use a sharp, notched knife.

Great Outdoors Skillet Cornbread

CLASSIC DESSERT GETS A MAKEOVER WORTHY OF A YELLOWSTONE COWBOY THANKS TO DOWN-HOME CORNBREAD.

PREP TIME 15 MINUTES
COOK TIME 30 MINUTES
YIELD MAKES 8 SERVINGS

INGREDIENTS

- 1 tsp butter
- ¾ cup half-and-half
- 1 egg, beaten
- ½ cup vegetable oil
- 1 tsp pure vanilla extract
- 1 cup cornmeal, preferably Ramona Farms
- 1 cup all-purpose flour
- 2 tsp baking powder
- ½ tsp baking soda
- ¼ cup granulated cane sugar
- ½ tsp salt
- ½ cup roasted corn kernels

DIRECTIONS

1. Preheat the oven to 350 degrees F. Butter the bottom and sides of a 9-inch cast iron skillet.

2. In a medium mixing bowl, combine the half-and-half, egg, oil and vanilla. In a separate bowl mix together the cornmeal, flour, baking powder, baking soda, sugar and salt.

3. Make a well in the middle of the dry mixture and pour in the wet mixture. Fold the ingredients together, then add the roasted corn and mix gently to combine. Pour batter into the prepared cast iron skillet and bake for 25 to 30 minutes until a toothpick or knife inserted in the center comes out clean. Cut into wedges and serve warm with Clover Honeycomb Compound Butter.

CLOVER HONEYCOMB COMPOUND BUTTER

Serve this with your favorite biscuits or use it to cook your sweets: either way, you won't be disappointed.

INGREDIENTS

- 2 Tbsp raw clover honeycomb, room temperature
- 1 stick butter

DIRECTIONS

1. Lay a thin piece of honeycomb the same length as the butter on top of a piece of plastic wrap big enough to cover the butter completely on all sides.

2. Lay the butter on top of the honeycomb. Lay another thin piece of honeycomb on top of the butter. Wrap one side of plastic wrap over and around the sides of the stack. Then wrap the sides over the top.

3. Gently squish the honeycomb so that the butter is covered evenly on all sides. Refrigerate until firm, about an hour. Carefully unwrap (it will be very sticky!). Slice with a sharp, wet knife and serve.

Mountain Oysters

THIS DELICACY IS A STAPLE OF CALF CASTRATION SEASON (YUP, THEY'RE TESTICLES: NOT OYSTERS) AS FEATURED ON *YELLOWSTONE* SEASON 1. THIS RECIPE WAS GRACIOUSLY PROVIDED BY THE FAMED MOUNTAIN OYSTER CLUB'S EXECUTIVE CHEF, OBIE HINDMAN.

PREP TIME 5 MINUTES
WAIT TIME 4–8 HOURS
COOK TIME 10–12 MINUTES
YIELD 28-30 COINS

INGREDIENTS

- ¼ cup salt
- 1 quart warm water
- 1 lb mountain oysters, peeled (ask your butcher to peel them), sliced into ½-inch-thick coins
- Vegetable oil
- 4 cups all-purpose flour
- 2 Tbsp cumin
- 2 Tbsp white pepper
- 2 Tbsp onion powder
- 1 Tbsp kosher salt
- 1 Tbsp chili powder blend
- 4 Tbsp paprika

DIRECTIONS

1. Dissolve the salt in the warm water. Add the coins and soak in the refrigerator for 4 to 8 hours or overnight.

2. Fill a medium heavy-bottom pot or Dutch oven with 2 inches of vegetable oil. Heat oil to 350 degrees F. Use a deep frying thermometer to keep the temperature consistent.

3. Whisk remaining ingredients in a large mixing bowl until well combined.

4. Place half of the coins in the flour mixture and agitate them with your hand, rubbing them between your fingers to create a craggy crust. Carefully place them one by one into the hot oil and fry until they float, then another 30 seconds to get them nice and crispy.

5. Remove from the oil to a paper towel-lined tray or plate. Repeat. Serve immediately with cocktail sauce and lemon.

TIPS FROM THE TRAIL

Lemon and cocktail sauce are the traditional accoutrements for this conversation-starting app, but you're welcome to serve with your favorite dipping sauces if you need a bit more flavor.

Bison Nachos

IN ADDITION TO BEING A SEMINAL PART OF WESTERN HISTORY
(SHEA BRENNAN OF *1883* COULD TELL YOU ALL ABOUT THE MASSIVE
BISON HUNTS OF THE 19TH CENTURY) THE BISON ALSO HAPPENS
TO MAKE FOR EXCEPTIONAL EATING.

PREP TIME 15 MINUTES
COOK TIME 10 MINUTES
YIELD 4–6 SERVINGS

INGREDIENTS

- 1 lb ground bison
- 1 Tbsp olive oil
- 1 Tbsp tomato paste
- 1 Tbsp taco seasoning
- 1 Tbsp onion flakes
- 1 tsp fennel seeds
- ¼ cup water
- 1 (1-lb) bag corn tortilla chips
- 1 cup prepared queso sauce, warmed
- ½ cup prepared black beans, rinsed and drained
- 1 cup chunky pico de gallo salsa

DIRECTIONS

1. Brown the bison in olive oil in a large
skillet over medium heat. Drain any fat that
accumulates. Stir in the tomato paste, taco
seasoning, onion flakes and fennel seeds, then
stir in the water. Simmer on medium-low for
10 minutes.

2. Carefully arrange a base layer of chips
on a large plate or platter. Drizzle on a thin
layer of queso to hold the other ingredients
in place. Carefully stack remaining chips,
adding more cheese as you go to create a
mountain of nachos.

3. Spoon on meat, then beans,
then pico de gallo.

TIPS FROM THE TRAIL

This recipe calls specifically for
bison meat, but if you're unable
to find it, simply opt for the
highest quality beef you
can find, with a lean to
fat ratio of about 85:15.

Shake 'N Bake Dutt-Ritos

CAN YOU BUY THE ORIGINALS AT THE CORNER STORE? SURE—BUT THAT'S NOT THE DUTTON WAY. TO MAKE YOUR SNACK CHIPS WORTHY OF A *YELLOWSTONE* WATCH PARTY, YOU'VE GOT TO DO IT YOURSELF.

PREP TIME 15 MINUTES
COOK TIME 30 MINUTES
YIELD 144 CHIPS

INGREDIENTS

- ½ cup cheese powder, such as King Arthur Better Cheddar
- 1–2 Tbsp buttermilk powder
- 1 Tbsp tomato bullion, such as Knorr
- 1 Tbsp garlic powder
- 2 Tbsp onion flakes
- 2 Tbsp MSG
- 3 Tbsp kosher salt
- 2 Tbsp nutritional yeast
- 2 Tbsp smoked paprika, hot or mild
- 36 high-quality corn tortillas, quartered
  Olive oil spray

DIRECTIONS

1. Combine all the flavor powder ingredients in a resealable bag and shake to combine.
2. Preheat air fryer or oven to 300 degrees F.
3. Air fry or bake tortillas for 10 to 12 minutes or until very lightly browned and crispy. If using an air fryer, you will hear them flipping, which sounds like corn popping, when they are almost done.
4. Spray both sides of the chips lightly with olive oil, add in small batches to the bag of flavor powder and shake to coat. Gently tap each chip before removing from the bag to remove excess.
5. Store leftover powder in an airtight container.

TIPS FROM THE TRAIL

This recipe uses white cheddar powder. Use yellow cheddar if you want your chips to be more orange. Don't skip the MSG or nutritional yeast, which make these chips extra craveable. Use hot smoked paprika if you want an extra kick.

Season Premiere Maple Bacon Popcorn

TIRED OF THE SAME OLD BUTTER TOPPING ACCENTUATING YOUR FAVORITE *YELLOWSTONE* MOMENTS? MAKE YOUR NEXT VIEWING MORE MEMORABLE WITH THIS UNEXPECTED FLAVOR COMBO.

PREP TIME 5 MINUTES

COOK TIME 10 MINUTES

YIELD 1–4 SERVINGS

INGREDIENTS

- ½ cup popcorn kernels
- 3–4 Tbsp coconut oil
- 1 Tbsp butter or butter alternative
- 2 Tbsp maple syrup
- 1 tsp liquid smoke
- ¼ cup Bac-Os or other bacon bits
- 2 Tbsp nutritional yeast
- 1 tsp red pepper flakes, optional
- Salt to taste

TIPS FROM THE TRAIL

This recipe is perfect for experimentation. Want spicier popcorn? Add more red pepper flakes. Want a bit of zip? Add some lemon salt. The possibilities are endless.

DIRECTIONS

1. Pour the popcorn kernels into a large Dutch oven, stock pot or saucepan with a heavy lid. Stir in enough coconut oil to generously coat the kernels, about 3 to 4 tablespoons.

2. On medium heat, cover and cook until you hear a 2-second pause between pops, about 5 minutes.

3. Meanwhile, melt the butter and maple syrup over low heat or in a microwave. Stir in the liquid smoke and then pour the mixture over the fresh popcorn and toss to coat.

4. Stir in the bacon bits, nutritional yeast, crushed red pepper flakes if using and salt and toss again.

Meaner Than Evil BBQ Hot Wings

THE FIRE IN THESE WINGS WILL HELP YOU CHANNEL YOUR INNER BETH DUTTON. JUST BE CAREFUL YOU DON'T GET CARRIED AWAY IN THE HEAT OF THE MOMENT.

PREP TIME 15 MINUTES
WAIT TIME 2–4 HOURS
COOK TIME 20 MINUTES
YIELD 1–3 SERVINGS

INGREDIENTS

12   chicken wings
½   cup spicy barbecue sauce, (see pg. 167) or your favorite brand

SPICE RUB

1–2   Tbsp red pepper flakes
2   Tbsp brown sugar
2   Tbsp smoked hot paprika
1   Tbsp sea salt
¼   tsp black pepper

DIRECTIONS

1. Secure the chicken wings and the spice rub ingredients in a resealable bag. Shake to coat, then massage the spices into the chicken. Refrigerate for 2 to 4 hours.

2. Grill on medium, covered, turning occasionally, until thoroughly cooked with a nice char and crispy.

3. Brush both sides with barbecue sauce, return to the grill and let brown, about 2 to 5 minutes more.

4. Place the wings in a large bowl and toss with more barbecue sauce to coat.

AIR FRY 'EM UP

Alternatively, you can cook the wings in the air fryer. Spray the wings with vegetable oil then preheat it to 400 degrees F. Place the wings in the basket so that they are not touching, standing them on end against the walls if needed. Air fry for 18 to 20 minutes, turning halfway through and shaking occasionally, until thoroughly cooked and crispy or until an instant-read thermometer inserted into the wings reads 165 degrees F.

Crispy Doves

ONE OF THE STARS OF A MASSIVE SEASON 5 GAME PLATTER, THESE DOVES DON'T QUITE MAKE THE DUTTON DINNER TABLE PEACEFUL—BUT THEY SURE ARE DELICIOUS.

PREP TIME 15 MINUTES
WAIT TIME 8–10 HOURS
COOK TIME 15 MINUTES
YIELD 1–4 SERVINGS

INGREDIENTS

- 4 doves or quail
- 2 Tbsp olive oil or olive oil spray
- 1 Tbsp sugar
- 1 Tbsp sea salt
- 1 tsp paprika
- 1 tsp garlic powder
- 1 tsp onion powder
- 4 lemons, thinly sliced crosswise
- 4 small pats of butter

DIRECTIONS

1. Place the birds in a non-reactive lidded container. Spray or brush the birds with olive oil, then sprinkle them liberally all over with sugar, salt, paprika, garlic powder and onion powder.

2. Cover and refrigerate overnight.

3. Heat an air fryer or outdoor grill to 375 degrees F. Remove the birds from the marinade and discard liquid. Cover the inside of a grill-safe pan or air fryer basket with a layer of sliced lemons.

4. Lay the birds breast side down on top of the lemons, spray them with olive oil and cook for 7 minutes.

5. Flip the birds breast side up. Give them another spray of oil, lay a small pat of butter on each of their breasts and cook for 7 minutes longer or until an instant-read thermometer inserted into the thickest part of the birds reads 165 degrees F. Let rest for 5 minutes before serving with charred lemon slices.

TIPS FROM THE TRAIL

Small game birds like doves and squab are staples at wild-game restaurants like the historic Buckhorn Exchange in Denver.

A ranch dog resting in the bed of a pickup truck in West Yellowstone, Montana. Ranch dogs are employed in livestock herding but are generally gentle with their families.

THE PERFECT YELLOWSTONE WATCH PARTY

Ideas to make your next *Yellowstone* viewing event a party no one will ever forget.

PREGAME WITH YELLOWSTONE PARTY GAMES

IF ONE OF your posse is a natural gamemaster, have them write up a few rounds of trivia questions or charades prompts for before the show or during the commercials.

SERVE UP PITCHERS OF COWBOY COCKTAILS

KEEP IT SIMPLE with Coors Banquet (the Bunkhouse's beverage of choice) or the more old-school sarsaparilla and moonshine, or get creative with Western cocktails like a classic Ranch Water (tequila, lime juice and mineral water).

GET THE RIGHT DUDS

IMMERSE YOURSELF IN the culture of the series by enforcing a Western dress code for your party. Break out your most well-loved jean jacket, invest in a Stetson and dust off those cowboy boots. Just don't be surprised when everyone comes dressed as Rip.

WATCH THE SHOW AL FRESCO

IF YOU HAVE the space for it, there's no better way to watch *Yellowstone* than under a vault of stars. Rent or invest in a projector and screen, bundle up and make your watch party an event to remember.

ROAST MARSHMALLOWS OVER A CAMPFIRE

IF YOU HAVE the outdoor space for a firepit, make like you're in Big Sky Country and have a little at-home campout with all the trimmings. If you don't have that luxury, outdoor tabletop fire pits (open-topped table lighters producing a single contained flame just big enough to roast marshmallows over) can be found at reasonable prices.

GET ADVENTUROUS WITH YOUR APPS

ARE YOUR GUESTS brave enough to eat like real cowboys? Put them to the test with adventurous western delicacies like Mountain Oysters (pg. 58) or Rattlesnake Sausage Chowder (pg. 121). Daring fare immediately separates the courageous from the cowardly and makes for a great conversation starter.

SEE WHO'S PSYCHIC

HAVE EVERYONE WRITE down five predictions for the upcoming episode and seal them in envelopes. When the episode's over, see whose predictions were closest to the truth. Maybe the person with the fewest correct predictions gets to host the next viewing party?

CREATE SOME DUTTON-STYLE DRAMA

AFTER THE SHOW, take the *Yellowstone* spirit of conflict to the game table and create some drama with *Yellowstone* Monopoly, a Dutton-themed riff on the classic board game. If you're wondering which property gets the honor of the coveted Boardwalk position, it's the Dutton Ranch Main House, of course!

Yellowstone Lower Falls waterfall during sunset. The national park boasts nearly 300 waterfalls.

Chicken Fried Steak, pg. 98.

MAIN COURSES

The stars of your dinner table will outshine the brightest stars in Big Sky Country—or Hollywood, for that matter.

Cowboy Coffee-Rubbed Bison Rib-Eyes

ASK ANYONE IN THE BUNKHOUSE AND THEY'LL TELL YOU THAT COWBOY COFFEE IS THE BASIS FOR A GOOD DAY OF WORK. WE TOOK THAT SPIRIT AND USED COFFEE BEANS TO INFUSE EXTRA FLAVOR INTO THIS STEAK.

PREP TIME 15 MINUTES
WAIT TIME 1 HOUR
COOK TIME 1 HOUR
YIELD 2–4 SERVINGS

INGREDIENTS

- ¼ cup coffee beans
- 1 Tbsp coarse sea salt
- 1–2 small-to-medium dried red chiles, hot or mild, destemmed
- 1 tsp black peppercorns
- 2 lb bison tomahawk or bone-in rib-eye (you can also substitute beef)
- 1 Tbsp neutral high-heat cooking oil, such as avocado or canola

DIRECTIONS

1. Place the coffee, salt, chile(s) and peppercorns into a resealable bag and smash with a meat mallet to make a rub. Alternatively, grind to a coarse texture using a mortar and pestle.

2. Coat steaks evenly with the rub, pressing it firmly into the meat. Let sit until it reaches room temperature, about an hour.

3. Preheat the oven to 275 degrees F. Place the steak on a baking sheet with a wire cooking rack. Cook until steaks reach an internal temperature of 135 degrees F for medium (which is 10 degrees less than the final temperature of 145) about an hour, depending on thickness.

4. Heat a cast-iron griddle or comal over high heat. Add the oil, then sear for 1 to 2 minutes per side or until a blackened crust forms.

5. Serve immediately: no resting is needed with reverse searing.

REVERSE PSYCHOLOGY

Reverse searing the steak takes a bit longer to cook but seals in the seasoning. Plus, "low and slow" cooking is recommended for bison. Coffee helps tenderize the steaks while adding flavor, and the caffeine makes this an excellent choice for a hearty breakfast steak.

Jefferson River Grilled Trout

YELLOWSTONE TAKES PLACE IN THE HEART OF FLY-FISHING COUNTRY (JUST ASK ROARKE). WHETHER YOU'VE CAUGHT IT YOURSELF OR LET SOMEONE ELSE DO THE ANGLING, THIS SIMPLE FISH DINNER IS SURE TO PLEASE.

PREP TIME 5 MINUTES
COOK TIME 15–20 MINUTES
YIELD 4 SERVINGS

INGREDIENTS

- 4 dressed trout, heads and tails intact
- 1 lemon, thinly sliced
- 4 sprigs rosemary
- ¼ cup olive oil
- Coarse sea salt to taste

DIRECTIONS

1. Lay each trout on the center of a piece of aluminum foil that is slightly longer and wider than the fish.
2. Stuff each cavity with lemon slices and a sprig of rosemary, then drizzle the skin with olive oil and sprinkle with salt.
3. Place the foil with the trout on a grill over medium and cook for 15 to 20 minutes or until fish is firm to the touch and the skin peels easily away from the flaky flesh.

1923 GIN RICKEY

This prohibition-era cocktail is featured in *1923*'s barroom scene, and is just as classic as a grilled fish dinner.

INGREDIENTS

- 2 oz Old Tom gin
- 2 Tbsp freshly squeezed lime juice, about 1 lime
- ½ cup sparkling water or seltzer
- Lime wedge, for serving
- 1 oz simple syrup (optional)

DIRECTIONS

Fill a cocktail shaker with ice, then add the gin, simple syrup and lime juice. Shake vigorously until the outside of the shaker becomes frosty, then strain into a Collins glass and top with sparkling water. Garnish with a lime wedge.

TIPS FROM THE TRAIL

According to *Farmers' Almanac*, the high water content of fish makes it difficult to get a good sear, so make sure your grill is super hot before cooking.

Beth's Gourmet Hamburger (or Tuna) Helper

THIS IS NOT YOUR TYPICAL HAMBURGER HELPER OUT OF THE BOX. BETH USES HER BIG BRAIN TO ANALYZE AND ELEVATE BOXED HAMBURGER HELPER INTO A GOURMET CASSEROLE, A TRICK YOU CAN NOW REPLICATE.

BETH'S GOURMET HAMBURGER HELPER WITH HAMBURGER

PREP TIME 5 MINUTES
COOK TIME 35 MINUTES
YIELD 4 SERVINGS

INGREDIENTS

- 1 lb ground beef
- 1½ cups beef or vegetable stock
- 2 cups milk
- 1 Tbsp dried onion flakes
- 2 Tbsp oregano, divided
- 1 box Hamburger Helper, Deluxe Cheeseburger Macaroni
- 1 cup marinara sauce, such as Rao's
- 1 cup shredded Italian blend cheese, divided
- ½ cup panko or other breadcrumbs

DIRECTIONS

1. Preheat the oven to 350 degrees F.
2. Brown beef over medium heat in a nonstick skillet breaking up the meat. Drain fat.
3. Stir in stock, milk, onion flakes, 1 Tbsp of oregano and seasoning packet. Boil, add pasta, reduce to a simmer and cook for 10 minutes.
4. Stir in marinara and ½ cup cheese. Transfer to 34-oz oven-safe baking dish.
5. Sprinkle ½ cup cheese, breadcrumbs and remaining oregano over the top.
6. Bake for 20 minutes.

BETH'S GOURMET HAMBURGER HELPER WITH TUNA

PREP TIME 5 MINUTES
COOK TIME 35 MINUTES
YIELD 4 SERVINGS

INGREDIENTS

- 1 (12-oz) can evaporated milk
- 1 cup chicken or vegetable broth
- 1 box Hamburger Helper, Deluxe Cheeseburger Macaroni
- 2 (5-oz) cans tuna, drained
- 1 Tbsp dried onion flakes
- ½ cup Italian blend shredded cheese
- ½ cup panko or other breadcrumbs
- 1 tsp oregano

DIRECTIONS

1. Preheat the oven to 350 degrees F.
2. Combine the evaporated milk, broth and seasoning in a saucepan and bring to a boil over medium heat.
3. Add the macaroni, reduce heat to a simmer and cook 10 minutes, stirring occasionally. Remove from heat.
4. Stir in the tuna and onion flakes then transfer to a 34-oz oven-safe baking dish. Sprinkle cheese, breadcrumbs and oregano over the top.
5. Bake for 20 minutes or until lightly browned.

Branding Iron Grilled Cheese Sandwiches

YOU DON'T HAVE TO HAVE A BRAND AS WELL-KNOWN AS YELLOWSTONE'S HOOKED ROCKING Y TO ENJOY THIS DRAMATIC TAKE ON A LUNCHTIME CLASSIC. BUT IT HELPS.

PREP TIME 10 MINUTES
COOK TIME 12–15 MINUTES
YIELD 4 SERVINGS

INGREDIENTS

- 8 large slices bread
- 2 Tbsp butter, melted
- ½ tsp garlic powder
- 1 cup shredded Parmesan
- ½ cup goat cheese, softened
- 4 oz sliced mozzarella, preferably buffalo
- 4 oz sharp cheddar, shredded or sliced

DIRECTIONS

1. Preheat the oven to 350 degrees F.
2. Brush both sides of the bread with melted butter, then sprinkle with garlic powder. Spread the insides with goat cheese.
3. Top 1 slice of bread with slices of mozzarella and cheddar then top with the other slice of bread, goat cheese side down.
4. Grease an oven-safe skillet (cast-iron preferred) with the remaining melted butter, then toss a Tbsp or 2 of Parmesan cheese in the bottom of the pan.
5. Set the sandwich on top of the Parmesan in the pan, then pile the rest of the Parmesan on top. Bake for 12 to 15 minutes or until all the cheese is melted and the top of the sandwich is nicely browned.
6. Heat a food-safe branding iron in an open fire until it turns gray then, wearing heavy heat-proof gloves, carefully imprint your brand on the surface of the bread.

THE PERFECT GRILLED CHEESE

Some people believe that grilled cheese must be made on the stovetop or over an open flame, but the secret to a perfectly melty grilled cheese sandwich is toasting it in the oven instead of over a burner. Use the best quality sandwich bread you can find, with a firm crust and a tight crumb (meaning the bread doesn't have a lot of holes in it) so the brand can be seen clearly on the surface of the bread.

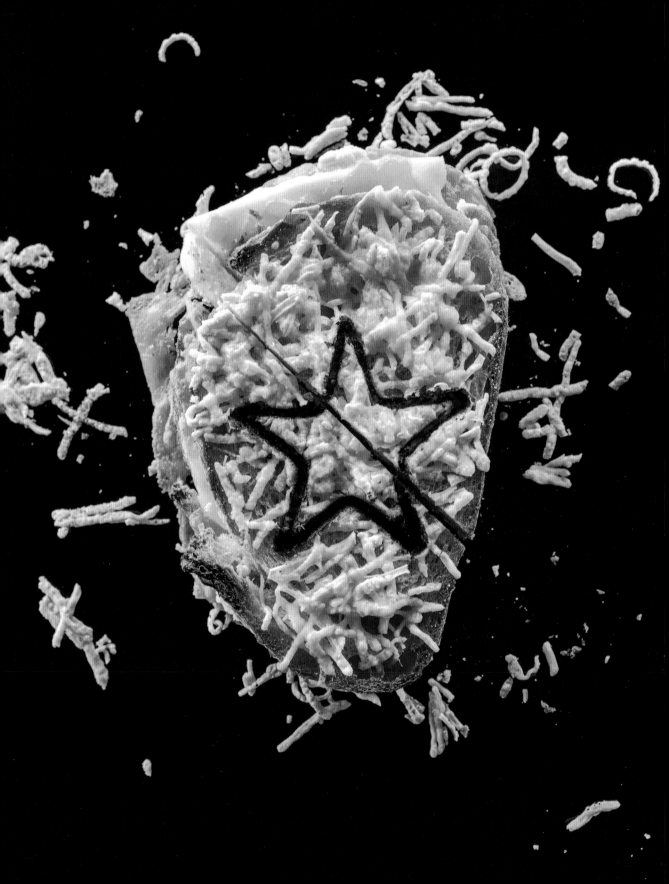

Auction Day Tri-Tip Sandwich

AUCTION DAY ON *YELLOWSTONE* HAS A TENDENCY TO CONTAIN A BIT MORE EXCITEMENT THAN THE BIG SALE: BETTER LOAD UP ON SOME COWBOY-STYLE ENERGY FIRST.

PREP TIME 15 MINUTES
WAIT TIME 1–8 HOURS
COOK TIME 50 MINUTES
YIELD 4 SERVINGS

INGREDIENTS

- ⅓ cup finely ground kosher salt
- ⅓ cup finely ground black pepper
- ⅓ cup garlic powder
- 1 tri-tip roast, about 2 lb
- 4 soft white sandwich rolls
- 1 cup salsa

DIRECTIONS

1. Combine the salt, pepper and garlic powder to make a rub, then press the rub into the tri-tip, coating completely on all sides. Cover and refrigerate for at least an hour or overnight.

2. Place the grate of an outdoor grill close to the flames and preheat to high. Set the meat directly above the flames to sear, about 5 to 8 minutes per side.

3. Turn the grill to medium and/or raise the grate as high as it will go. Continue to cook, turning occasionally, for 25 to 30 minutes or until the temperature on an instant-read thermometer reads 145 degrees F for medium rare.

4. Remove from heat and let sit for 10 minutes before slicing. Pile thin slices of tri-tip and a layer of salsa between a sliced roll.

TIPS FROM THE TRAIL

Tri-tip steak is known for its distinctive marbling, flecks of fat that melt into the steak as it cooks. So don't skimp on the steaks!

Jamie's Grilled Octopus

YELLOWSTONE'S RESIDENT IVY LEAGUER SITS DOWN TO SOME PROVERBIAL HUMBLE PIE IN SEASON 2 IN THE FORM OF GATOR'S DELICIOUS GRILLED OCTOPUS.

PREP TIME 15 MINUTES

COOK TIME 1 HOUR

YIELD 4–6 SERVINGS

INGREDIENTS

- 2   bay leaves
- 2   Tbsp sea salt
- 1   medium whole octopus, about 2 lb
- 3   large lemons, divided
- 6–8   large romaine lettuce leaves
- 2   cups chopped scallions
- 2   cups chopped tomatoes
- 2   Tbsp olive oil
- 1   tsp Greek seasoning blend

DIRECTIONS

1. In a large stockpot, boil enough water to submerge the octopus. Add bay leaves and salt and reduce to a simmer.

2. Add the octopus and cook until tender, about 45 minutes. Remove, drain and slice off the legs.

3. Zest and juice 2 of the lemons.

4. Heat a grill or grill pan to high. Place the octopus on the grill and cook for 2 to 3 minutes on each side.

5. Cover a large platter with romaine leaves, then spoon on the chopped scallions and tomatoes. Arrange the grilled octopus on top. Drizzle with olive oil and lemon juice, then sprinkle with Greek seasoning blend and lemon zest. Cut remaining lemon into halves to serve.

VODKA AND THREE OLIVES

Don't call this a martini. Beth wouldn't approve.

INGREDIENTS

- 3   oz Tito's vodka
- 3   extra-large pimento-stuffed green olives
    Bamboo skewers

DIRECTIONS

Spear olives onto a bamboo skewer and place inside a chilled martini glass. Fill a cocktail shaker with ice, add the vodka and shake vigorously until the outside of the shaker becomes frosty. Strain into the glass.

TIPS FROM THE TRAIL

Exactly how long you boil
your octopus will depend on the
size of the animal. As you cook it,
gently poke the meat with
a fork every 15 minutes
until tender.

The Best Salisbury Steak in Montana

WHAT ELSE IS THERE TO SAY EXCEPT "YOU ENJOY IT"?

PREP TIME 15 MINUTES
WAIT TIME 8 HOURS
COOK TIME 40 MINUTES
YIELD 4 SERVINGS

INGREDIENTS

- 8 saltine crackers
- 1 large egg, lightly beaten
- ½ tsp sea salt
- 1 tsp granulated garlic
- 1 Tbsp onion flakes
- 1 Tbsp grainy Dijon mustard, such as Grey Poupon
- 1 Tbsp Worcestershire sauce
- 1 tsp fish sauce such as Red Boat
- ¼ tsp freshly ground black pepper
- 1 lb ground beef, preferably grass-fed
- 1 Tbsp butter, for cooking

POLENTA

- 1 cups water
- 1 tsp kosher salt
- 1 cup polenta, such as Regina Farms parched stone milled
- 1 Tbsp butter

MUSHROOM SAUCE

- 1 Tbsp butter
- 1 Tbsp all-purpose flour
- 1 cup beef broth or stock
- 1 Tbsp tomato paste
- 1 tsp grainy Dijon mustard, such as Grey Poupon
- 1 Tbsp Worcestershire sauce
- 1 tsp fish sauce such as Red Boat
- 1 cup prepared roasted mushrooms, see pg. 37
- Freshly ground black pepper to taste

DIRECTIONS

1. Place the saltines in a resealable bag and crush them into crumbs with your hands or a meat mallet.

2. Combine the saltines, egg, salt, garlic, onion, mustard, Worcestershire sauce, fish sauce and black pepper into the beef and mix well with your hands or a rubber spatula. Divide into 4 portions, then form into football-shaped patties. Cover and refrigerate 4 to 8 hours or overnight.

3. Remove from refrigerator and let sit for 15 minutes at room temperature.

4. Start the polenta: Bring water and salt to a boil in a large saucepan and slowly add polenta while whisking constantly until there are no lumps.

5. Reduce heat to medium-low and simmer, whisking often, until polenta starts to thicken, about 5 minutes. Cover and cook for 30 minutes, whisking frequently until it's too thick to whisk, then continue stirring with a rubber spatula until the texture is creamy and the grains are tender. Stir in butter.

6. While the polenta is cooking, heat 1 Tbsp of butter in a large skillet over medium heat and cook the patties for 8 to 10 minutes on each side or until browned. Transfer to a plate.

7. Reduce the heat to low. Add 1 Tbsp of butter to skillet then whisk in the flour to combine, followed by the broth, tomato paste, mustard, Worcestershire sauce and fish sauce. Stir to combine then add the mushrooms.

8. Spoon an equal portion of polenta onto each plate. Top with Salisbury steak and mushroom sauce.

Cider-Braised Turkey Thighs

THIS RECIPE FOR CIDER-BRAISED TURKEY THIGHS, TYPICAL OF NATIVE CUISINE, IS REPRINTED WITH PERMISSION FROM *THE SIOUX CHEF* BY SEAN SHERMAN. SHERMAN'S COOKBOOK, *THE SIOUX CHEF'S INDIGENOUS KITCHEN*, IS AVAILABLE WHEREVER BOOKS ARE SOLD.

PREP TIME 15 MINUTES + 12 HOURS FOR RICE
COOK TIME 1 HOUR
YIELD 4 SERVINGS

INGREDIENTS

- 3 Tbsp sunflower oil
- 2-3 lb turkey thighs, skin removed
- 1 cup chopped wild onion
- 1 cup corn, wild rice or game stock
- ½ cup cider
- ¼ cup maple or apple cider vinegar
- 2 whole juniper berries
- 4 sage leaves
- 1 large apple, cored and diced
  Black Wild Rice, see below

NOTE: IF YOU CAN'T FIND WILD ONION, SUBSTITUTE THE WHITE PARTS OF SCALLIONS. SAVE THE LIQUID LEFT OVER FROM THE WILD RICE TO USE AS PART OF THE STOCK.

DIRECTIONS

1. Heat the oil over medium-high heat in a Dutch oven or heavy pot. Brown the thighs on all sides, about 3 to 4 minutes per side. Remove and set aside. Reduce the heat to medium, add the onion and cook until softened.

2. Add the stock and cider and bring to a boil, scraping any browned bits from the pan.

3. Stir in the remaining ingredients and return the thighs to the pot. Reduce the heat to a simmer. Cover the pot and cook the turkey, turning occasionally, adding more stock if the liquid becomes low, until the turkey is very tender, about 45 minutes.

4. Remove turkey from the pot and set aside, covered. Skim the fat from the surface of the liquid, bring to a boil and reduce the liquid by half. Taste and adjust the seasoning. Serve the thighs over Black Wild Rice.

BLACK WILD RICE

PREP TIME 5 MINUTES
COOK TIME 30–40 MINUTES
YIELD 4 SERVINGS

INGREDIENTS

- 1 cup black rice or other wild rice
- 1 cup water
- 2 cups poultry or vegetable broth or stock

DIRECTIONS

Rinse the rice, cover with water and let soak overnight. Drain. Bring 1 cup of water and the stock to a boil in a large saucepan. Stir in the rice, reduce the heat to medium and simmer for 20 to 30 minutes or until tender, firm and chewy, but not crunchy.

Longhorn Carne Asada Burritos

ACCORDING TO LEGEND, THE BURRITO WAS INVENTED BY MEXICAN COWBOYS (VAQUEROS) TO EAT ON THE TRAIL. THEY COULD BE PREPARED AHEAD AND EATEN WITH ONE HAND, MAKING THEM THE PERFECT ON-THE-GO FOOD.

PREP TIME 20 MINUTES
COOK TIME 10 MINUTES
YIELD 2–4 SERVINGS DEPENDING ON TORTILLA SIZE

INGREDIENTS

- 1 **Tbsp sea salt**
- ⅛ **tsp dried Mexican oregano, optional but recommended**
- ⅛ **tsp red chile powder**
- ⅛ **tsp garlic powder**
- 1 **lb ⅛-to-¼-inch-thick skirt steak or bottom round steak**
- 1 **squirt bottle filled with about ½ cup pineapple juice**
- 4 **large (10–12 inch or larger) high-quality flour tortillas**
- 1 **cup Cowboy Beans (see pg. 146), warmed and drained**
- 1 **cup finely shredded cabbage**
  Salsa for serving

DIRECTIONS

1. Preheat grill to 500 degrees F.
2. Combine salt, oregano, chile powder and garlic powder in a small bowl.
3. Pat the steaks dry with a paper towel, then sprinkle generously on both sides with the seasoning.
4. Sear the steaks on 1 side for about a minute; flip the steak before you start to see the juice on the surface. Sear on the other side for another minute. Squirt roughly 1 Tbsp of pineapple juice on the steak, flip and repeat on the other side. Flip the steak again to caramelize the meat. Let steak rest for 1-2 minutes.
5. Thinly slice the meat against the grain, then dice into ¼-inch pieces.
6. Place the tortillas on a large flat surface. Layer the chopped carne asada, beans and cabbage down the middle of each tortilla, leaving about ½ inch of space on either side and an inch or 2 at the top and bottom.
7. Roll the base and filling 1 turn up so that the fold is in the center/widest part of the tortilla. Then fold the 2 shorter ends in and roll again until the filling is fully enclosed. Wrap in foil until ready to eat. Serve with salsa on the side.

Chicken Fried Steak

JIMMY'S BIG TEXAS DINNER OF CHICKEN FRIED STEAK LOOKED SO
GOOD ON THE SHOW, WE DECIDED TO GO OUT AND GET THE EXACT
PLATE IT'S SERVED ON TO RECREATE THE LOOK.

PREP TIME 20 MINUTES
COOK TIME 30 MINUTES
YIELD 4 SERVINGS

INGREDIENTS

- 1½ cups all-purpose flour
- 1 tsp kosher salt
- 1 tsp ground black pepper
- 1 tsp garlic powder
- 1 tsp onion powder
- 1 tsp paprika
- 2 cups buttermilk
- 1 egg
- 4 (4–5 oz) cube steaks
- Sea salt
- Mashed potatoes and gravy (see pg. 160)
- Prepared green beans

DIRECTIONS

1. Whisk together the flour, salt, pepper, garlic powder, onion powder and paprika in a pie pan or other shallow, rimmed dish.

2. Whisk together buttermilk and egg in a shallow, rimmed pan.

3. Place a steak in the flour mixture and flip to coat. Shake any excess back into the dish. Dip into the buttermilk mixture to coat, then dip it back in the flour mixture. Place the steak on a wire rack to dry a bit. This will help the batter stay on while frying. Repeat with the other 3 steaks.

4. Heat an inch of vegetable oil to 350 degrees F in a Dutch oven.

5. Place a steak in the oil and cook until the top begins to brown, about 5 to 7 minutes. Very carefully flip to avoid cracking the coating and cook for 4 to 5 minutes.

6. Remove from the oil, sprinkle with sea salt and let dry on a clean wire rack. Repeat with the remaining steaks.

7. Serve with peppered country gravy, mashed potatoes and green beans.

DID YOU KNOW?

It's generally accepted that the first chicken fried steaks were made in Texas by German and Austrian immigrants who were adapting their familiar schnitzel dishes.

Smash Burgers With Bourbon Braised Onions

HAVE SOME LEFTOVER GROUND BEEF FROM THE BEST SALISBURY STEAK IN MONTANA (PG. 93)? WHIP UP SOME SMASH BURGERS FOR LUNCH AND PLEASE THE WHOLE CREW.

PREP TIME 20 MINUTES
COOK TIME 1½ HOURS
YIELD 4 SERVINGS

SPECIAL EQUIPMENT
Smashed burger press
Kitchen scale
Firm metal spatula

INGREDIENTS

BOURBON BRAISED ONIONS
2 Tbsp butter
1 large, sweet onion, very thinly sliced
¼ cup sweet bourbon such as Jim Beam Honey Bourbon Whiskey

SECRET SAUCE
¼ cup mustard
¼ cup ketchup
¼ cup sweet pickle relish
¼ cup mayonnaise
2 Tbsp white vinegar

SMASH BURGERS
4 potato hamburger buns
1 Tbsp melted butter
1 lb ground beef
Kosher salt to taste
8 slices cheese, such as sharp cheddar or American

DIRECTIONS
1. Melt 2 Tbsp butter in a large skillet over medium-low. Stir in the onions, then cook, stirring occasionally, until very soft and lightly browned.
2. Add the whiskey and cook for 10 to 15 minutes more or until the edges of the onions are brown and starting to crisp and the liquid is absorbed. Turn the heat to high and cook for 1 minute. Remove from the heat, set aside and keep warm.
3. Stir together Secret Sauce ingredients. Refrigerate until needed.
4. Brush the buns, inside and out, with melted butter, then toast them.
5. Roll the beef into 2-oz balls. Heat a griddle over high heat. Do not add oil. Place a ball of meat on the griddle and immediately press it as flat as possible with the press and hold it there for 1 minute. Then slide the press to the side and off the burger while still pressing down.
6. Sprinkle the burger with salt, then carefully scrape it off the griddle and flip it with a firm metal spatula. Immediately top with 2 slices of cheese then scrape the burger off the griddle and place it on the bottom half of a bun. Repeat the process to make a double or triple burger.
7. Spoon a dollop of the secret sauce over the top then pile on a portion of the onions and the top of the bun. Repeat with remaining burgers.

Barrel Racers' Pulled Pork

AT THE RODEO, ONE OF THE FASTEST-PACED EVENTS IS BARREL RACING, AND IF YOU'RE LIKE MIA OR LARAMIE, IT'LL GIVE YOU QUITE AN APPETITE FOR CLASSIC BBQ.

PREP TIME 30 MINUTES
COOK TIME 5–6 HOURS
YIELD 10–12 SERVINGS

INGREDIENTS

RUB
- ¼ cup turmeric
- ¼ cup mild red chile powder
- ¼ cup sea salt
- 1 Tbsp garlic powder
- 1 Tbsp ground black pepper
- 1 Tbsp dried oregano
- 1 Tbsp mustard powder
- 2 Tbsp onion powder
- 2 Tbsp ground cinnamon
- 10 dried juniper berries, crushed

PULLED PORK
- 1 pork butt, about 5 lb

COOKING LIQUID
- 2 Tbsp high heat vegetable oil such as avocado or canola
- 2 cups chicken stock
- 1 cup red wine vinegar
- 1 cup maple syrup
- 1 cup bourbon whiskey
- 1 Tbsp liquid smoke

DIRECTIONS

1. Preheat the oven to 300 degrees F.

2. Whisk together all rub ingredients in a medium bowl. Rub the mixture all over the pork, pressing the spices in as you go. The rub will turn into a paste.

3. Heat a Dutch oven over medium. Add the oil. Brown the pork on all sides, about 2 to 3 minutes per side.

4. Add chicken stock and red wine vinegar, then stir and scrape any browned bits from the bottom of the pan with a wooden spoon. Reduce heat to medium-low and whisk in the maple syrup, whiskey and liquid smoke.

5. Place the pork butt in the pan, fat side up. Cover and transfer to the oven. Cook for 4 hours. The pork will be just starting to turn tender. Remove the lid and cook for 1 hour longer.

6. Transfer pork to a large cutting board or bowl, leaving the liquid in the Dutch oven. Boil the liquid over medium heat until it is reduced by half. Meanwhile, shred the pork with 2 large forks.

7. Stir the shredded pork into the reduced liquid. Season with salt and pepper to taste and serve with coleslaw.

Oregon Trail Dutch Oven Short Ribs

THE DUTCH OVEN WAS A STAPLE BIT OF COOKWARE FOR THE FOLKS WHO SETTLED THE WEST, LIKE JAMES DUTTON AND HIS FAMILY, BECAUSE A DUTCH OVEN CAN BE PLACED DIRECTLY IN THE BURNING COALS OF A CAMPFIRE. OR, YOU CAN USE YOUR STOVE: YOUR CHOICE.

PREP TIME 10 MINUTES
COOK TIME 1½ HOURS
YIELD 2–4 SERVINGS

INGREDIENTS

- 2 Tbsp high-heat cooking oil, such as avocado or canola
- 3½ lb short ribs, approximately 8 pieces
- 3 cups beef broth
- 1 cup red wine
- 2 Tbsp tomato paste
- 2 tsp Worcestershire sauce
- 8 carrots
- 2 sprigs thyme
- 2 sprigs rosemary
- 2 Tbsp balsamic vinegar
   Salt and pepper to taste

DIRECTIONS

1. Preheat oven to 325 degrees F.

2. Heat 2 Tbsp oil in a large Dutch oven over high heat. Sear the short ribs on all sides, about 2 minutes per side or until a deep brown crust forms. Remove and set aside.

3. Add the broth to the pan then stir and scrape any browned bits from the bottom of with a wooden spatula or spoon. Reduce the heat to medium. Stir in the red wine, tomato paste and Worcestershire sauce.

4. Return the ribs to the pot, arrange the carrots, thyme and rosemary around the ribs and bring to a boil, then reduce the heat to medium-low so that the liquid is just simmering and cover.

5. Cook for 1 hour or until the meat is very tender, checking periodically to see if you need to add more broth.

6. Remove the meat, carrots and sprigs from the liquid, then add the balsamic vinegar, bring to a boil and cook until the liquid is reduced by half. Remove sprigs. Taste and add salt and pepper if needed.

7. Arrange the meat and carrots on plates and spoon the sauce over the top.

Firepit Staked Salmon

THERE'S NO BETTER WAY TO ENJOY YOUR FRESH CATCH THAN TO COOK IT UP RIGHT THERE BY THE RIVERSIDE USING THIS TRADITIONAL METHOD.

PREP TIME 5 MINUTES
COOK TIME 1 HOUR
YIELD 4 SERVINGS

INGREDIENTS
- 1 lb salmon fillets, divided into 3–5-oz portions
- Sea salt and pepper to taste

DIRECTIONS
1. While the fire is heating, wet the stakes then spear the salmon against the grain. Push the stakes into the ground, pointy side up and with the skin side facing the flame, very close to the flames but not close enough so that they catch fire.

2. Cook for 15 minutes, then turn the flesh side to the fire. Cook for about 45 minutes more or until the desired degree of doneness is achieved. Carefully remove the stakes from the fire and the salmon from the stakes. Season with salt and pepper.

STAKE TO TRADITION
Staking over an open flame is a traditional Native American method for cooking salmon. You will need a roaring campfire and untreated wooden stakes, preferably redwood, with pointed tips. Oak, hickory and maple are good choices for firewood. And always be sure that when your campfire is doused, you leave your campsite exactly the way you found it.

TIPS FROM THE TRAIL
To make sure your camp fire doesn't produce too much smoke, avoid burning any damp or green wood so you can taste the meat, not the heat.

Cara Dutton's Irish Stout Pot Roast

THE LARGELY SCOTCH-IRISH SETTLERS OF THE AMERICAN WEST, LIKE THE DUTTONS, BROUGHT ANCESTRAL RECIPES WITH THEM, MAKING EMERALD ISLE-INSPIRED FARE LIKE THIS COMMON.

PREP TIME 15 MINUTES
COOK TIME 3½–4 HOURS
YIELD 8–10 SERVINGS

INGREDIENTS

1	Tbsp celery salt
1	Tbsp granulated garlic
1	Tbsp dried onion flakes
1	Tbsp coarsely ground black pepper
2½–3	lb bottom round roast
1	large white onion, thinly sliced, about 2 cups
2–3	cups beef broth or stock, divided
8–10	new potatoes
1	large, fat carrot, scrubbed and cut into ½-inch pieces
24	oz Irish stout, such as Guinness
4	cloves garlic, chopped
2	Tbsp Worcestershire sauce
1	Tbsp granulated cane sugar
3	(3-inch) sprigs fresh rosemary
1	tsp arrowroot powder or corn starch

DIRECTIONS

1. Stir together the celery salt, garlic, onion flakes and black pepper in a small bowl.

2. Rub the mixture all over the meat.

3. Lay the roast with the fattiest side down in a large Dutch oven heated to high on the stovetop. Cook for 4 to 5 minutes to render some of the fat off, then turn the meat and brown on all the other sides for 3 to 4 minutes. Remove meat from pot and set aside.

4. Preheat the oven to 325 degrees F.

5. Reduce the stovetop to medium. Add the onions to the pot and cook in the remaining fat until browned, about 10 minutes. Pour in 1 cup of broth and scrape up any browned bits stuck to the bottom of pot.

6. Place the meat in the middle of the Dutch oven, fat side down. Surround it with the potatoes and carrots. Stir in the Irish stout, garlic, Worcestershire sauce, sugar and enough additional broth so that the liquid covers half of the meat. Toss in the rosemary sprigs then cover and place in the oven. Cook for 2 hours, turning and basting the meat once an hour and adding more broth as needed to keep the meat halfway submerged. After 2 hours, stir in the arrowroot or corn starch to thicken the sauce. Cook for an hour or 2 longer or until the sauce has the color and consistency of chocolate sauce and the meat shreds easily.

Herd of American bison grazing in Yellowstone National Park. The name Yellowstone refers to yellow sandstone.

THE BEST YELLOWSTONE FOOD MOMENTS

The Duttons' dinner table is the setting for some of the series' most dramatic moments, and food in general plays a special role in the lives of the Yellowstone ranch family. Here are a few of our favorite moments of culinary drama.

TATE'S DONUT

SEASON 1, EPISODE 6

WHEN TATE INTERRUPTS a conversation between the grown-ups, John Dutton employs a classic grandpa trick that is just as classically not appreciated by Monica. To finish the conversation without any little eavesdroppers, John employs a bit of psychology he knows the boy can't refuse: he sends Tate to get himself a conspicuously large donut.

JAMIE AND THE OCTOPUS

SEASON 2, EPISODE 3

AS JAMIE DUTTON learns in his first abortive political campaign, government is a strange, many-tentacled beast. So when he withdraws from the race and returns to Yellowstone with his tail between his legs to sit down at the dinner table with the family, it's only natural that the Duttons are eating grilled octopus. Beth, of course, finds the image hilarious.

BETH STABS JAMIE UNDER THE TABLE

SEASON 2, EPISODE 4

AT DINNER WITH Jamie, his girlfriend Cassidy and the Dutton family, Beth creates a particularly cruel mess when she manipulates the seating arrangements to place herself next to Jamie. Before long, she's surreptitiously stabbed Jamie under the table with a blunt knife, affecting one of her most interesting dinner disruptions.

See recipe on PG. 26

See recipe on PG. 90

RIP MAKES BREAKFAST

SEASON 3, EPISODE 2

BETH DUTTON IS a character who has largely managed to close herself off emotionally from the rest of the world. Burdened with guilt, anger and hatred, we rarely see her with her guard down. That's why when she wakes up to find that Rip has made her breakfast, Beth has such a touching emotional response. You can recreate the fry bread Rip makes using the recipe on pg. 20.

GATOR GETS REJECTED

SEASON 3, EPISODE 9

GATOR IS AN exceptional (if protein-forward) cook and an extremely loyal member of the Dutton apparatus. This is why Tate and John's small betrayal of the Yellowstone chef might be one of the most memorable in the series. Despite the gourmet breakfast Gator has prepared, Tate—as kids will do—says he'd prefer a bowl of his favorite cereal, Choco Chimps. John, amused, sends a dejected Gator back into the kitchen for two bowls of the sugary treat.

BETH'S HAMBURGER HELPER

SEASON 4, EPISODE 1

BETH AND RIP'S domestic bliss in Season 4 begins with Beth "really getting this whole cooking thing." Her first offering as a chef is one shared by many a latchkey kid and frustrated home cook: Hamburger Helper. Beth earnestly offering up something so pedestrian as an act of love is a rare, relatable look at the Dutton bulldog's softer side.

See recipe on PG. 85

See recipe on PG. 141

BEHIND THE SCENES: SHOW GATOR SOME LOVE!

AFTER THREE SEASONS of watching Gator prepare luxurious feasts only for the Duttons to storm off halfway through the meal, Yellowstone fans had had enough. They took to the internet, demanding to know why Gator kept having to endure these insults to his cuisine. Luckily, Gator, a real-life chef, is also in charge of cooking for the entire cast and crew: So even though the Duttons might waste food, Gator certainly doesn't.

THE SALAD WITH FRUIT IN IT

SEASON 4, EPISODE 8

THE DINNER TABLE is a sacred totem for John Dutton. When his family is complete, sitting around the table and enjoying Gator's cooking, all is right with the world. Sometimes this sacred quality associated with the dinner table is a serious matter, but it's especially memorable when it's played for laughs. When Beth has Gator make a salad containing prostate-friendly fruits, the traditionalist Rip is appalled. John's response: "Yes, they're good for the prostate. Lots of things are, but we don't talk about them at the dinner table."

A VEGAN RUINS DINNER

SEASON 5, EPISODE 5

IN A CLASSIC example of "Nobody's right when everybody's wrong," a Dutton dinner is cut short (shocking, we know) when Summer, critical of Gator's meal and abrasive in her veganism, and Beth start to fight. Summer points out that the only fare on the table is 47 different kinds of meat. Beth points out that Summer is insulting the Dutton way of life at their own table. A fistfight on the lawn ensues, broken up only when Rip pulls the two apart.

A large herd of elk dominates the landscape in the National Elk Refuge, Wyoming. Turn to pg. 40 for a recipe featuring this type of wild game.

Bunkhouse Chili (With Beans), pg. 130.

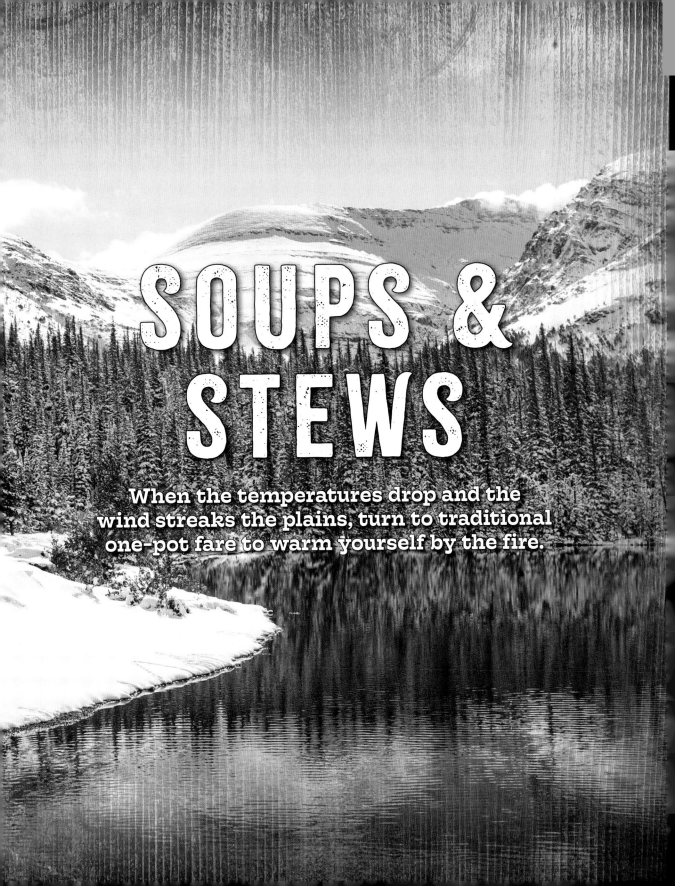

SOUPS & STEWS

When the temperatures drop and the wind streaks the plains, turn to traditional one-pot fare to warm yourself by the fire.

Rattlesnake Sausage Chowder

THIS SPICY CHOWDER HAS A BITE, BUT AT LEAST IT WON'T TAKE A BITE OUT OF YOU. DON'T SOURCE THE SNAKE YOURSELF, PLEASE: NO NEED TO STOMP IT TO DEATH, TATE-STYLE.

PREP TIME 10 MINUTES
COOK TIME 20 MINUTES
YIELD 4–8 SERVINGS

INGREDIENTS

- 2 Tbsp olive oil
- 2 cups halved fingerling potatoes
- 4 rattlesnake sausage links, cut into ½-inch coins
- ½ cup bourbon whiskey
- 32 oz vegetable or chicken stock
- 1 can sweetened condensed milk
- 2 cups shredded sharp cheddar cheese
- 1 large jalapeño or 2 medium serrano chiles, thinly sliced
- Salt to taste

DIRECTIONS

1. Heat the olive oil in a large Dutch oven or heavy-bottomed soup pot over medium heat. Fry the potatoes cut side down with sausage until browned, about 3 to 5 minutes, flipping the sausages halfway through. Remove from the pot and set aside.

2. Pour the whiskey and stock into the pot and bring to a boil. Using a wooden spatula, scrape up any brown bits stuck to the bottom of the pot.

3. Reduce the heat to medium-low and stir in the condensed milk and cheddar until the cheese is completely incorporated into the liquid, about 3 minutes.

4. Add the peppers, sausage and potatoes and simmer on low for 10 minutes or until the potatoes are fork tender. Taste and salt if needed. Serve immediately.

A BONEY BUSINESS

We definitely recommend buying pre-made rattlesnake sausage links: apart from the safety factor, working with a whole snake involves removing the tasty backstrap-like dorsal muscle from a myriad of rib bones.

Easy Green Pozole With Smoked Turkey or Pheasant

A LARGE PORTION OF U.S. CATTLE COUNTRY WAS PART OF MEXICO UNTIL THE MID-1800s, WHICH IS WHY SO MUCH OF COWBOY TRADITION IS INFUSED WITH MEXICAN INFLUENCE—LIKE THIS DELICIOUS POZOLE.

PREP TIME 5 MINUTES
COOK TIME 20 MINUTES
YIELD 4–6 SERVINGS

INGREDIENTS

- 32 oz chicken stock
- 16 oz prepared roasted green chile salsa with tomatillos, jarred or fresh
- 2 cups prepared shredded smoked turkey or pheasant
- 1 (25-oz) can hominy, drained or 2–3 cups fresh hominy
- 1 Tbsp Mexican oregano
- 2 cups shredded cabbage
- 1 cup loosely packed cilantro leaves
- 4 green onions, chopped
- 4 radishes, sliced
- 2 limes, cut into wedges

DIRECTIONS

1. Bring the stock to a boil in a large soup pot. Stir in salsa, meat, hominy and oregano. Simmer for 20 minutes. Ladle into bowls.
2. Serve shredded cabbage, cilantro, green onions, radishes and limes on the side for topping.

1883 PUNCH

A classic alcoholic punch as featured in *1883*.

INGREDIENTS

- 4 tsp sugar
- 32 oz boiling water
- 8 oz whiskey

DIRECTIONS

Dissolve the sugar into the boiling water. Let cool. Pour in the whiskey and stir well to combine. Serve at room temperature or over ice.

FUN FACT

Mexican oregano is not really oregano at all: It's a relative of lemon verbena native to the Americas. Look for it in the spice section of your local market or online. If you can't find it, substitute marjoram.

Teeter's Sum Bits Stew

TRADITIONALLY KNOWN AS SON-OF-A-BITCH STEW, ANY RECIPE THAT STARTS WITH THE INSTRUCTIONS "KILL OFF A YOUNG STEER" IS GOING TO BE INTENSE, AS TEETER PROVES IN SEASON 4.

PREP TIME 20 MINUTES
COOK TIME 7-8 HOURS
YIELD 6-8 SERVINGS

INGREDIENTS

- ½ lb beef cheeks
- ½ lb beef foot
- 1 set marrow gut
- ½ lb sweetbreads, soaked in water for 3 hours to remove impurities
- 1 lb fatty stew meat
- 1 Tbsp red wine vinegar
- 1 tsp salt
- ½ tsp pepper
- 1 Tbsp hot sauce, plus more for serving

DIRECTIONS

1. Cut all the beef parts into 1-inch pieces then add to a slow cooker with enough water to cover everything and cook on low for 7 to 8 hours.
2. Let cool overnight in the refrigerator then remove the white fat cap formed over the top. Underneath that will be the jelly-like collagen, which you want to keep. Return the stew to the slow cooker and heat on low for 2 more hours. Add remaining ingredients and serve.

TIPS FROM THE TRAIL

Teeter makes her Sum Bits Stew in a slow cooker, a fact revealed in the closed captioning for the episode.

Corn Masa and Sage Dumplings in Partridge Soup

A TYPICAL DISH ENJOYED BY MONTANA'S NATIVE TRIBES, THESE SAVORY MORSELS MAKE WILD GAME SOUP AN UNBELIEVABLE DELIGHT.

PREP TIME 10 MINUTES
COOK TIME 35 MINUTES
YIELD 4 SERVINGS

INGREDIENTS

- 2 large eggs
- 2 Tbsp olive oil
- 5 oz masa harina
- 1 tsp baking powder
- ¼ tsp sea salt
- ¼ tsp ground black pepper
- ½ tsp ground dried sage or 1 tsp chopped fresh sage
- 1 Tbsp chopped onion flakes
- 8 cups chicken stock
- 2 cups buttermilk
- 2 cups shredded partridge or quail

DIRECTIONS

1. Whisk together the eggs and oil for a minute or two until combined.
2. In another bowl, stir together the masa harina, baking powder, salt, pepper, sage and onion flakes. Stir the masa mixture into the egg mixture with a fork. Refrigerate for 15 minutes.
3. Meanwhile, in a large soup pot with a heavy lid, bring the stock, buttermilk and shredded meat to a boil, stirring constantly. Gently roll the chilled masa mixture into eight 1-inch balls and add to the boiling soup.
4. Reduce to a low simmer, cover tightly and cook for 30 minutes.

TIPS FROM THE TRAIL

Be sure to use masa harina instead of cornmeal or corn flour. Masa harina is treated in alkaline solutions that impart a distinct flavor you won't get from regular cornmeal.

Pinto Bean and Caramelized Ham Soup

THIS DISH HAS ROOTS IN THE SAME MONTANA RESTAURANT THAT INSPIRED THE SHEEPHERDERS' (PG. 53): IT'S CLEAR YELLOWSTONE'S HOME STATE SPECIALIZES IN CLASSIC, HEARTY FARE, LIKE THIS SAVORY SOUP.

PREP TIME 10 MINUTES
COOK TIME 2 HOURS
YIELD 4–6 SERVINGS

INGREDIENTS

- 1 medium onion
- 2 cups dried pinto beans
- 2 tsp sea salt
- 1 lb thick-cut ham steak, cooked
- 1 Tbsp melted butter
- 2 tsp light or dark brown sugar
  Croutons and red pepper salsa, for serving

TIPS FROM THE TRAIL

Be sure to use dried beans instead of canned. The broth produced by cooking the beans is the secret step to the success of this soup.

DIRECTIONS

1. Cut the onion in half across the middle so that the root remains intact. Peel off the outer skin. Place onions, beans and salt in a large soup pot and cover with 2 quarts of water. Bring to a boil and cook for 5 minutes then reduce the heat to simmer until the beans are soft, about 1½ to 2 hours. Add more water as needed so that the beans are fully submerged. There should always be about a ½ inch of water covering the beans.

2. While the beans are cooking, preheat the broiler to 475 degrees F. Brush one side of the ham steak with melted butter, then sprinkle with sugar. Broil until browned, about 3 to 5 minutes. Flip the ham and repeat the process. Let cool slightly then chop into ¼-to-½-inch pieces.

3. Once the beans are soft, stir in the ham and simmer for 10 more minutes, adding additional water if the soup starts to look too dry. Taste and add more salt if needed. Remove and discard the onion and ladle into bowls. Serve with croutons and red pepper salsa.

Chili Two Ways

IN THE SEASON 4 FINALE, THE BUNKHOUSE GETS INTO A HEATED
DEBATE OVER WHETHER OR NOT CHILI HAS BEANS. HERE'S A
RECIPE FOR EACH SO YOU CAN DECIDE FOR YOURSELF.

BUNKHOUSE CHILI (WITH BEANS)

PREP TIME 5 MINUTES
COOK TIME 15–20 MINUTES
YIELD 4 SERVINGS

INGREDIENTS

- 32 oz beef broth or stock
- 1 lb lean ground beef
- 1 large white onion, chopped
- 1 Tbsp unsweetened dark chocolate powder, such as King Arthur Baking Company Black Cocoa
- 1 Tbsp cinnamon
- 1 Tbsp turmeric
- 2–3 Tbsp red chile powder
- 1 tsp ground cloves
- 1 tsp smoked paprika
- 1 (15½-oz) can dark red kidney beans with liquid
- 1 (28-oz) can tomato puree
- ¼ cup apple cider vinegar
- 1–2 tsp liquid smoke
- 2 Tbsp Louisiana-style hot sauce, such as Frank's or Crystal, plus more for serving

DIRECTIONS

1. Bring the broth or stock to a boil in a large soup pot, stir in the ground beef, onions, chocolate, cinnamon, turmeric, chile powder, cloves and paprika and boil until the liquid is reduced by half, scraping down sides with a rubber spatula and breaking up any large pieces of meat, about 20 minutes.
2. Reduce the heat to low. Stir in the beans with their liquid, tomato puree, apple cider vinegar, liquid smoke and hot sauce. Cover and cook for 1 hour, stirring occasionally.

JIMMY WAS RIGHT (AKA CHILE COLORADO CON CARNE)

PREP TIME 5 MINUTES
COOK TIME 30 MINUTES
YIELD 4 SERVINGS

INGREDIENTS

- 1 (14-oz) container frozen red chile puree
- 2 Tbsp olive oil
- 1½ lb beef chuck, cut into 1-inch cubes
- 4 cloves garlic, minced
- 2–3 Tbsp masa harina, use more for a thicker sauce
- 1 Tbsp dried Mexican oregano
- ½ tsp sea salt
- 1 Tbsp red wine vinegar
- 1 tsp Worcestershire sauce
- 1 cup sour cream
- 1 cup shredded cheddar or jack cheese
- ½ cup chopped chives or scallions

DIRECTIONS

1. Run the container of chile puree under hot water to defrost slightly. Meanwhile, heat the olive oil in a large saucepan over medium heat. Remove the partially frozen disc of chile puree and place it on one side of the pan. (It will defrost and cook while the beef is browning.)
2. Add the beef and saute for 10 minutes or until cooked through and the chile is liquefied.
3. Reduce the heat to low, stir in the garlic, masa harina, Mexican oregano, salt, red wine vinegar and Worcestershire sauce. Cover and simmer for 15 to 20 minutes.
4. Add a dollop of sour cream and sprinkle with cheese and chives or scallions.

A grizzly and her two cubs take a walk among Willow Flats in Grand Teton National Park. A scene in which Rip kills a grizzly bear to protect tourists is based on a real-life account from Yellowstone National Park.

"Train Station" Funeral Potatoes, pg. 154.

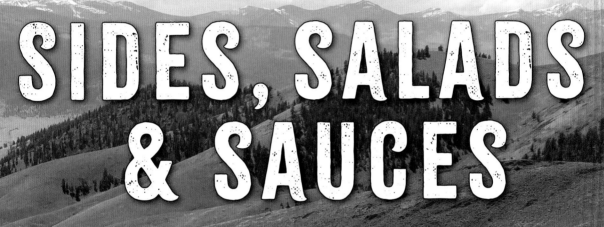

SIDES, SALADS & SAUCES

You've never seen Gator leave much empty space in the Dutton dining room. That's because any good country kitchen is well-stocked with everything you need to make all your fixings to fill out your table.

Deviled Egg Potato Salad

THE PERFECT MASH-UP OF TWO CLASSIC COOKOUT STAPLES, THIS POTATO SALAD IS SO HEARTY IT'S ALMOST A MEAL ON ITS OWN.

PREP TIME 20 MINUTES
COOK TIME 15 MINUTES
YIELD 8–10 SERVINGS

INGREDIENTS

- 2 lb Yukon Gold potatoes, quartered
- 6 hard-boiled eggs, smashed into bits by hand or roughly chopped
- 1 cup chopped celery
- ⅓ cup chopped red onion
- 3 Tbsp capers in liquid
- 3 Tbsp sweet pickle relish
- 3 Tbsp yellow mustard
- 1-2 Tbsp minced chipotle chiles in adobo sauce
- ⅔-1 cup mayonnaise, such as Duke's or Hellmann's
- 3 Tbsp apple cider vinegar
- ½ tsp ground turmeric
- 1 tsp dried dill
- 1 tsp Lawry's Seasoned Salt
- 1 tsp sugar
- 1 tsp coarse sea salt
- Black pepper to taste

DIRECTIONS

1. Boil the potatoes in water with ¼ tsp of salt until fork tender, about 15 minutes. Drain and let cool.

2. Mix remaining ingredients in a large mixing bowl and add the potatoes.

3. Transfer into another bowl so that the sauce that has accumulated on the bottom of the mixing bowl is now on top. Cover and refrigerate 2 hours to let the flavors meld.

TIPS FROM THE TRAIL

The same spices can be combined to make traditional deviled eggs instead, but we find this preparation is easier for a large group.

Stetson II Chopped Salad with Basil Ranch Dressing

A *YELLOWSTONE*-INSPIRED SPIN ON THE FAMOUS STETSON SALAD FROM COWBOY CIAO IN ARIZONA, THIS VERSION USES TRADITIONAL NATIVE AMERICAN HUUN GA'I (COB-ROASTED DRIED CORN KERNELS) AS A NOD TO THE BROKEN ROCK RESERVATION.

PREP TIME 45 MINUTES

YIELD 4 SERVINGS

INGREDIENTS

- 2 cups diced tomatoes
- 1 Tbsp balsamic vinegar
  Sea salt to taste
- 1 cup toasted sunflower seeds
- 1 cup dried sour cherries
- 1 cup dried blueberries
- 7 oz arugula, chopped
- 8 oz smoked trout
- 2 cups Huun Ga'i, such as Ramona Farms, prepared according to package directions
- 2 cups prepared pearl couscous
  Dutton Family Ranch Dressing, see pg. 167

DIRECTIONS

1. Combine the diced tomatoes and balsamic vinegar and season with sea salt to taste. Set aside.

2. Combine the sunflower seeds and dried fruit. Set aside.

3. Fill the bottom of a salad bowl with a layer of arugula.

4. Drain the liquid from the tomatoes. Arrange the smoked trout, berry mixture, Huun Ga'i, tomato mixture and couscous in sections on top. Toss with dressing.

TIPS FROM THE TRAIL

We find our Dutton Family Ranch to be the perfect dressing for this salad, but you're free to experiment with your favorites!

Dr. Stafford's Prostate-Friendly Salad With Fruits

YES: IT DOES HAVE FRUIT IN IT. BUT DON'T LET THAT STOP YOU FROM ENJOYING THE TASTE AND HEALTH BENEFITS OF THIS SALAD.

PREP TIME 15 MINUTES

YIELD 2–4 SERVINGS

INGREDIENTS

- 7 oz mixed greens
- ½ cup strawberries
- ½ cup blackberries
- ½ cup blueberries
- ½ cup pepitas
- 2 Tbsp olive oil
- 2 Tbsp white balsamic vinegar
  Ground black pepper and sea salt to taste
  Dash cayenne and/or Tajín seasoning to taste

DIRECTIONS

Toss the greens, berries and pepitas in olive oil. Drizzle with white balsamic, then sprinkle with salt, pepper, cayenne and Tajin.

WATERMELON MOONSHINE

The Lainey Wilson song featured in Season 5 is also a delicious cocktail to sip alongside this salad.

INGREDIENTS

- 1½ cups moonshine, or more if needed
- 4 cups watermelon chunks
  Lime wedges, for serving

DIRECTIONS

Stuff the watermelon chunks into a 24-to-32-oz mason jar with a lid and smash them down with a kitchen mallet to release the juice. Add enough moonshine to cover completely. Seal and let sit for 1 week, inverting the jar every other day. Refrigeration is optional. Serve strained over ice with lime wedges.

Lucky Cowboy Caviar

COWBOY CAVIAR WAS INVENTED IN THE 1940S BY HELEN CORBITT, HEAD CHEF AT THE ZODIAC ROOM AT DALLAS'S NEIMAN MARCUS DEPARTMENT STORE. IT'S THE PERFECT MIX OF SIMPLE COWBOY TASTE AND UPSCALE LIVING, JUST LIKE THE DUTTONS' BIG HOUSE.

PREP TIME 15 MINUTES
YIELD 6–8 SERVINGS

INGREDIENTS

- 1 lb black-eyed peas, prepared according to package directions
- ¼ cup diced jalapeño or serrano
- ½ cup diced red onion
- 1 cup diced yellow bell pepper
  Juice from 1 large lemon, about 3 Tbsp
- 1 Tbsp red wine vinegar
  Hot sauce to taste
  Tortilla chips for serving

DIRECTIONS

Combine all ingredients except chips in a large bowl. Refrigerate for an hour to let the flavors meld. Serve with chips for scooping.

TIPS FROM THE TRAIL

Some believe eating black-eyed peas brings good luck, and the Duttons' enemies can use all the luck they can get.

Hearty Greens With Whiskey Myers's Warm Bourbon Vinaigrette

THE MUSIC OF WHISKEY MYERS IS HEAVILY FEATURED IN *YELLOWSTONE*, WITH THE BAND EVEN MAKING A CAMEO IN SEASON 1, EPISODE 4. THE BOOZY DRESSING ON THIS SALAD IS A NOD TO THEIR HARD WORK ON THE SHOW.

PREP TIME 15 MINUTES
COOK TIME 15 MINUTES
YIELD 1–2 SERVINGS

INGREDIENTS

- 1 egg
- 2 strips bacon
- 2 Tbsp pure maple syrup
- 2 Tbsp bourbon whiskey
- 1 tsp honey mustard
- ½ oz dried or ½ cup sliced fresh chanterelle, oyster and/or porcini mushrooms
- 5 oz hearty greens such as spinach, kale and/or chard
-    Sea salt to taste
-    Freshly ground black pepper to taste
- 1 Tbsp minced shallots
- 1 clove garlic, minced
- ½ cup chopped bell pepper
- 2 Tbsp red wine vinegar
-    Ground sumac to taste

DIRECTIONS

1. Boil the egg for 8 minutes, then immediately plunge into a bowl of ice water to cool before peeling and slicing into 4 wedges. The centers should be slightly jammy.
2. Meanwhile, cook the bacon in a large skillet over medium until crispy. Let cool. Tear or cut into bite-size pieces. Remove all but 2 Tbsp of bacon grease from the pan.
3. Reduce the heat to low. Whisk in the maple syrup, whiskey and honey mustard.
4. Add the mushrooms and sauté until they soften, 3 to 5 minutes. Turn off the heat, add the greens and sauté until just starting to wilt, about 1 to 2 minutes.
5. Transfer to a large salad bowl. Immediately season with salt and pepper. Toss in the shallots, garlic, bell pepper and red wine vinegar. Season with salt and pepper to taste, then arrange on plates and garnish with sliced eggs. Sprinkle with ground sumac.

PARENTAL GUIDANCE

Though minimal, most of the alcohol in the salad dressing remains after cooking. Do not serve to children or anyone who would be negatively impacted.

Cowboy Beans

DRIED BEANS—EASILY PORTABLE, EASILY COOKED AND REQUIRING NO MORE THAN A SINGLE POT—HAVE BEEN A STAPLE OF LONG CATTLE RUNS SINCE LONG BEFORE THE DUTTONS MADE THEIR WAY WEST.

PREP TIME 15 MINUTES
COOK TIME 3 HOURS
YIELD 6–8 SERVINGS

INGREDIENTS

- 1 head garlic
- 1 (16-oz) bag dried pinto beans
- 2 quarts water
- 2 tsp sea salt, or more to taste
- ½ cup diced fresh tomatoes
- ¼ cup minced red onion
- 2 Tbsp red wine vinegar
- 2 Tbsp onion flakes
- 1 Tbsp Mexican oregano
- 1 Tbsp tomato paste

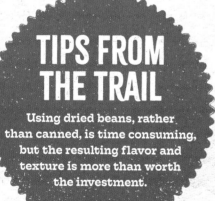

TIPS FROM THE TRAIL

Using dried beans, rather than canned, is time consuming, but the resulting flavor and texture is more than worth the investment.

DIRECTIONS

1. Smash the head of garlic (root side up) against a cutting board with the side of a chef's knife to separate the cloves, then smash each clove individually to remove the skins and crush the cloves a bit. Reserve 3 cloves. Coarsely chop the rest.

2. Pour the beans and water into a large Dutch oven or stock pot, covering the beans by 2 inches. Stir in the chopped garlic and salt. Bring to a boil, then reduce to medium and simmer uncovered until beans are soft, 1½ to 2 hours. If the water evaporates during cooking, gently add more water so that the beans are always completely submerged. Do not stir.

3. Once the beans are soft, mince the remaining 3 garlic cloves and add them to the pot along with the tomatoes, red onion, vinegar, onion flakes, Mexican oregano and tomato paste.

4. Simmer uncovered over low heat, stirring occasionally, for about 30 minutes to reduce the liquid. The beans should be slightly saucy, not soupy. Sample and add more seasoning to taste, then cover with a heavy lid, remove from heat and let sit for about 10 minutes to allow the flavors to meld.

Gun Barrel Mac and Cheese

WITH ITS CYLINDRICAL SHAPE AND ABILITY TO PACK A REAL WALLOP, IT'S EASY TO SEE WHY WE GAVE THIS MAC AND CHEESE A COWBOY-INSPIRED NAME. SHARPSHOOTER SHEA BRENNAN WOULD BE PROUD.

PREP TIME 15 MINUTES
COOK TIME 30 MINUTES
YIELD 4–6 SERVINGS

INGREDIENTS

- 1 lb ziti
- 2 cups cream
- 2 Tbsp butter
- 1 tsp salt
- 2 tsp grainy mustard such as Grey Poupon
- ¼ tsp cayenne
- 1 oz blue cheese, crumbled
- 2 oz Gruyère, shredded
- 2 oz white Irish cheddar, such as Dubliner, shredded
- ½ cup grated Parmesan
- 1 cup crumbled garlic-Parmesan croutons

NOTE: SHRED THE CHEESE YOURSELF, OTHERWISE THE SAUCE WILL BE GRAINY.

DIRECTIONS

1. Cook the pasta in salted water until it's al dente. Drain but do not rinse.
2. Heat the cream over medium-low until it just starts to simmer. Stir in the butter, salt, mustard and cayenne. When the butter is melted, start to gradually stir in the cheeses, stirring continuously until melted.
3. Preheat the oven to 350 degrees F.
4. Stir in pasta to coat. Divide the mixture between 4 to 6 ramekins. Sprinkle generously with Parmesan and croutons. Bake for 15 to 20 minutes or until browned.

DID YOU KNOW?

Elbow-shaped macaroni was invented in 1872 but might not have been readily available in 1883. Kraft processed cheese was invented 1916. During the Great Depression, Grant Leslie in Missouri sold pasta with a packet of cheese attached via rubber band, and a quick dinner staple was born.

"Trilobite" Hasselback Sweet Potatoes

A VISUAL TRIBUTE TO THE FOSSILS FOUND IN YELLOWSTONE THAT HELPED KICK OFF THE WEST'S PALEONTOLOGY CRAZE, WHICH HAS CAUSED SOME GRIEF FOR RANCHERS LIKE THE DUTTONS WHEN DIGGERS DISRUPT THEIR LAND, THESE HASSELBACK SWEET POTATOES MIGHT LOOK STRANGE, BUT THEY'RE DELICIOUS.

PREP TIME 20 MINUTES
COOK TIME 1 HOUR
YIELD 4 SERVINGS

INGREDIENTS

- 1 cup mixed nuts such as pistachios, walnuts, almonds and/or pecans
- 4 unpeeled sweet potatoes or yams
- 2–3 Tbsp melted butter
- 1 tsp pure vanilla extract
- 1 Tbsp ground cinnamon
- ½ cup granulated cane sugar
- Coarse sea salt to taste

DIRECTIONS

1. Put the nuts in a resealable plastic bag and smash them with a kitchen mallet.

2. Preheat the oven to 425 degrees F. Line a baking sheet with a baking mat or parchment paper.

3. Lay each potato down on its flattest side. Cut a series of slits through each potato, about ⅛ to ¼ inch apart, stopping about ¾ of the way down so that the slices all stay attached.

4. Stir together the melted butter and vanilla extract. Brush the potatoes with the butter mixture, making sure to get some in between the slices.

5. Bake for 45 minutes. Remove from the oven and gently run a fork across the tops of the potatoes to separate the slices a bit, then spoon nuts into the crevices and over the top and sprinkle generously with cinnamon, sugar and salt.

6. Bake for 15 to 20 minutes more.

The Roosevelt Lodge's Famous Baked Beans

THE ROOSEVELT IS A YELLOWSTONE NATIONAL PARK LODGE BUILT IN 1920 AND NAMED AFTER THEODORE ROOSEVELT, THE FATHER OF THE NATIONAL PARKS AND A FIGURE WHO STILL LOOMS LARGE OVER THE WEST IN ALL ITS DEPICTIONS.

PREP TIME 15 MINUTES
COOK TIME 45 MINUTES
YIELD 8–12 SERVINGS

INGREDIENTS

- 8 oz ground beef or uncased sausage
- 1 medium onion, diced
- 8 oz bacon, chopped to ¼-inch pieces
- 1 (16-oz) can pork and beans
- 1 (15-oz) can kidney beans, drained
- 1 (15-oz) can butter beans, drained
- 1 (15-oz) can lima beans, drained
- ½ cup brown sugar
- 2 Tbsp apple cider vinegar
- 1 Tbsp spicy brown mustard
- 1 tsp garlic powder
- ¼ tsp black pepper

NOTE: RECIPE USED WITH PERMISSION FROM YELLOWSTONE NATIONAL PARK. THE PARK IS NOT AFFILIATED WITH THE SHOW.

DIRECTIONS

1. Preheat the oven to 325 degrees F.
2. Sauté the meat with the onions in a large oven-safe skillet or Dutch oven. Drain the fat then stir in remaining ingredients and bake for 45 minutes.

TIPS FROM THE TRAIL

While ground beef is the more traditional cowboy protein option for this dish, we love the flavor added by sausage.

"Train Station" Funeral Potatoes

COMFORT FOODS THAT ARRIVE IN A CASSEROLE DISH ARE SO UBIQUITOUS AT SOMBER GATHERINGS THEY'RE KNOWN AS FUNERAL POTATOES IN SOME PARTS OF THE COUNTRY. THIS VERSION IS A COWBOY-INSPIRED SPIN BASED ON *YELLOWSTONE*'S SIGNATURE EUPHEMISM FOR WHEN SOMEONE'S NEXT STOP IS SIX FEET UNDER.

PREP TIME 10 MINUTES
COOK TIME 1 HOUR
YIELD 8–10 SERVINGS

INGREDIENTS

- 1 (30-oz) package hash browns, defrosted if frozen
- 2 Tbsp onion flakes
- 1 tsp garlic powder
- ½ tsp kosher salt
- 1 (10½-oz) can condensed cream of mushroom soup
- 1 cup plain Greek yogurt or sour cream
- 2 cups shredded sharp cheddar cheese, divided
- 1 Tbsp butter
- 1 bag Baked Ruffles Cheddar and Sour Cream potato chips, crushed*

*minus the few you "had to" eat while making this recipe

DIRECTIONS

1. Preheat the oven to 350 degrees F.
2. Combine the hash browns, onion flakes, garlic powder, salt, soup and yogurt or sour cream along with 1½ cups of cheddar cheese in a large mixing bowl.
3. Grease a 13-by-9-inch baking pan with butter. Add potato mixture and bake for 40 to 45 minutes or until the top is bubbling and starting to brown.
4. Remove, top with the remaining cheese then the chips and bake for 15 minutes more. Let cool for 10 minutes.

Sweet Grilled Acorn Squash

THE "THREE SISTERS" OF NATIVE AMERICAN COOKING WERE TRADITIONALLY BEANS, CORN AND SQUASH, WITH ACORN SQUASH BEING A PARTICULARLY POPULAR VARIETY. GET IN TOUCH WITH YOUR LAND'S ROOTS BY TRYING THIS NATIVE-INSPIRED RECIPE.

PREP TIME 10 MINUTES
COOK TIME 10 MINUTES
YIELD 4 SERVINGS

INGREDIENTS

  Olive oil spray
1 large acorn squash
½ cup melted butter
2 Tbsp pure maple syrup
1 tsp cinnamon
2 tsp Tajín
¼ tsp cayenne, optional

DIRECTIONS

1. Spray the grates with olive oil and heat the grill to medium. Halve the acorn squash lengthwise. Scoop out the seeds with a spoon and discard. Lay each half of the squash flesh-side-down and cut crosswise into ½-inch crescents.

2. Combine the melted butter, maple syrup, cinnamon, Tajin and cayenne if using. Brush one side of the squash slices with the butter mixture, then lay them butter side down on the grill before brushing the mixture on the other side.

3. Cover and cook until dark grill marks appear and the squash has softened, about 5 to 10 minutes per side. Transfer to a serving platter and drizzle any remaining butter sauce over the top. Serve immediately.

TIPS FROM THE TRAIL

There's no need to peel acorn squash before cooking. The edible skin softens significantly while cooking.

Old Faithful BBQ Twice Baked Potatoes With Crispy Skins

JUST AS THE NATIONAL PARK'S FAMOUS GEYSER CAN BE COUNTED ON TO SPOUT RIGHT ON CUE, THIS NO-FRILLS CLASSIC WILL RELIABLY PLEASE YOU AND YOURS.

PREP TIME 15 MINUTES
COOK TIME 1 HOUR 10 MINUTES
YIELD 4–8 SERVINGS

INGREDIENTS

- 4 russet potatoes
- 1 Tbsp olive oil
- ½ cup coarse sea salt
- 2 Tbsp butter
- ½-¾ cup barbecue sauce, see pg. 167
- ¼ cup sour cream
- 4 scallions, chopped
- ½ cup bacon bits, plus more for garnish
- 1 Tbsp grated Parmesan

DIRECTIONS

1. Preheat the oven to 350 degrees F.
2. Poke the potatoes several times with a fork to prevent them from exploding in the oven, then massage them all over with olive oil and roll them in a bowl filled with salt until they are evenly coated.
3. Lay the potatoes directly on the oven rack and bake for an hour. Let cool then cut them in half lengthwise with a large serrated knife.
4. Carefully scoop out the white filling, leaving the skin intact. Dump the innards in a mixing bowl. Mash in the butter, barbecue sauce, sour cream, scallions and bacon bits. Taste and add more barbecue sauce if needed. It will vary depending on the size of the potatoes. Spoon the filling back into the potato skins. Sprinkle with Parmesan.
5. Put the stuffed potato halves on a baking sheet lined with a wire rack. Return to the oven and bake for 15 minutes longer.

Smoky Mashed Potatoes With Sausage Gravy

AT THE DUTTON DINNER TABLE, SUMMER POINTS OUT THAT GATOR'S MASHED POTATOES HAVE BUTTER AND BACON GREASE IN THEM. WHILE THAT MIGHT NOT PLEASE ANY VEGANS, IT CERTAINLY MAKES FOR DELICIOUS EATING.

PREP TIME 20 MINUTES

COOK TIME 30 MINUTES

YIELD 10–12 SERVINGS

INGREDIENTS

- 5 lb Yukon Gold potatoes, cut into 1-to-2-inch chunks
- 2 (32-oz) containers vegetable broth or stock
- 10 cloves garlic, minced
- 2 Tbsp chopped onion flakes
- 2 Tbsp red chili powder
- 2 Tbsp bacon grease
- 2 cups broth retained from cooking the potatoes
- 4 Tbsp butter, preferably grass-fed
- 1 Tbsp diced chipotle chiles in adobo sauce
- 1 tsp liquid smoke
- 1 Tbsp smoky barbecue seasoning such as Stubb's BBQ Rub
- ½ tsp Arizona Habanero seasoning or other hot chili powder, optional

  Flaky salt and freshly ground black pepper to taste

GRAVY

- 1 packet of McCormick Peppered Country Gravy Mix
- 2 cups broth retained from cooking the potatoes
- 4 sausage patties (turkey, plant-based, pork, etc.) cooked and crumbled

DIRECTIONS

1. Place potatoes in a Dutch oven.

2. Add broth/stock, garlic, onion flakes, chili powder, bacon grease and enough water to cover potatoes.

3. Bring to a boil, then reduce the heat to medium and simmer uncovered until potatoes are very soft, about 25 minutes.

4. Drain potatoes and broth into a colander. Reserve broth. Return potatoes to Dutch oven and reduce heat to low.

5. Add about 2 cups of the potato broth, a half cup at a time, along with the butter. Smash the potatoes into the broth until you reach the desired consistency. Stir in the diced chipotle, liquid smoke, barbecue seasoning and habanero seasoning (if using). Taste, then season with salt and ground pepper. Add more barbecue seasoning and/or butter if desired.

6. Empty the gravy mix into a small saucepan. Whisk in 2 cups of the potato broth, replacing the milk suggested in the packaging directions. Stir in the sausage and heat according to the package instructions.

7. Add a generous portion of potatoes to a large plate. Make a well in the middle with a serving spoon and fill with gravy. Garnish with salt, pepper and a shake of barbecue seasoning.

Wedge Salad

SOMETIMES THE REST OF THE MENU IS SO HECTIC (LIKE WHEN GATOR PACKS THE TABLE WITH 40+ MEATS) THAT YOU NEED A NEW TWIST ON A CLASSIC STEAKHOUSE SIDE THAT COMES TOGETHER IN NO TIME.

PREP TIME 15 MINUTES
YIELD 4 SERVINGS

INGREDIENTS

- 1 head iceberg lettuce
- 1 cup crumbled blue cheese, divided
- ¼ cup olive oil
- ½ cup red wine vinegar
- 1 Tbsp grainy Dijon mustard
- ½ cup chopped candied pecans
- ½ cup bacon bits
- Salt and pepper to taste

DIRECTIONS

1. Wash the lettuce by yanking out the hard core, filling the crevices with water and then draining the whole thing upside down in a big bowl. Chop lengthwise into four wedges.

2. Place ¼ cup blue cheese in a bowl with oil and vinegar. Smash the cheese into the liquid with a fork to make a chunky paste. This will help distribute more blue cheese flavor throughout the salad. Then, whisk in the mustard.

3. Plate each wedge and drizzle with dressing, being sure to get it into all the cracks and crevices. Sprinkle on the remaining blue cheese, pecans and bacon bits. Season with salt and pepper.

TIPS FROM THE TRAIL

While you're certainly within your rights to use packaged "bacon" bits, you'll create much more flavor by crisping up your own fresh bacon and crumbling it.

"Mmmm, That's How You Make Biscuits" Biscuits

THIS DENSE BUT PILLOWY BREAKFAST STAPLE MADE IT OUT WEST VIA SOUTHERNERS SETTLING ITS VAST ACRES, AND BOY ARE WE GLAD THEY DID.

PREP TIME 20 MINUTES
COOK TIME 15 MINUTES
YIELD 12–15 SERVINGS

INGREDIENTS

- 2 cups all-purpose flour, plus more for rolling out the dough
- 4 tsp baking powder
- ½ tsp baking soda
- 1 tsp salt
- 4 Tbsp butter, cut into ¼-inch cubes
- ⅓ cup Greek yogurt
- 1 cup buttermilk
- 1 egg

DIRECTIONS

1. Preheat the oven to 450 degrees F. Mix the flour, baking powder, baking soda and salt together.

2. Add the butter, then squish and pinch the butter into the mixture. Place the bowl in the freezer.

3. In another bowl, whisk together the yogurt, buttermilk and egg.

4. Remove the flour mixture from the freezer, make a small well in the middle and pour in the wet mixture. Mix with a rubber spatula.

5. Roll out the dough on a well-floured work surface using a floured rolling pin to a ¼-to-½-inch-thick rectangle. Sprinkle it with flour, then fold it into thirds like a letter. Pat the dough down to make another rectangle the same size, sprinkle it with a bit of flour, then fold it like a letter again. Repeat the pat, sprinkle and fold a third time.

6. Cut the dough with a 2-inch cookie or biscuit cutter. Place on an ungreased 18-by-13-inch rimmed half-sheet baking pan and cook until browned, about 15 minutes.

TIPS FROM THE TRAIL

Make sure to use cold butter to produce the flaky layers that mark a true Southern-style biscuit.

COCKTAIL SAUCE

PREP TIME 15 MINUTES
CHILL TIME 1–2 HOURS
YIELD 16 SERVINGS

Serve this homemade version of a classic alongside your Mountain Oysters (pg. 58).

INGREDIENTS

- 1 cup Heinz chili sauce
- ¼ cup Heinz ketchup
- 3 Tbsp Atomic Extra Hot Horseradish or other extra-hot prepared horseradish
- 1 Tbsp Worcestershire sauce
  Juice from ½ lemon, about 1 Tbsp
  Tabasco sauce to taste

DIRECTIONS

Combine all ingredients. Mix and chill for 1 to 2 hours before serving.

TIPS FROM THE TRAIL

In a pinch? You can make a quick alternative to cocktail sauce by mixing equal parts sriracha and mayonaise.

HONEY HUCKLEBERRY BARBECUE SAUCE

PREP TIME **15 MINUTES**
COOK TIME **5 MIMUTES**
YIELD **16 SERVINGS**

Barbecue sauce is a bunkhouse classic, whether it's on pulled pork, brisket, burgers or potato chips. This version pays tribute to the intermixing of Anglo and Native cultures in the West by incorporating huckleberries.

INGREDIENTS

1⅓ cup tomato paste
1 cup white vinegar
⅓ cup huckleberry preserves
¼ cup clover honey
1 tsp hickory liquid smoke

2 tsp smoked paprika
2 tsp kosher salt
2 tsp ground cinnamon
1 tsp black pepper

DIRECTIONS

Combine all ingredients in a small saucepan, bring to a simmer over medium and cook for 5 minutes, stirring occasionally.

DUTTON FAMILY RANCH DRESSING

PREP TIME **10 MINUTES**
CHILL TIME **1–2 HOURS**
YIELD **16 SERVINGS**

This dressing is heavy on buttermilk and fresh herbs, making it as green as the Dutton ranch's un-grazed (and clover-free) pastures.

INGREDIENTS

1 cup buttermilk
⅓ cup plain Greek yogurt
⅓ cup mayonnaise such as Duke's or Hellman's
1 cup loosely packed fresh basil
½ cup loosely packed parsley
½ tsp fresh or dried dill
½ tsp celery salt
2 Tbsp chopped chives

1 small shallot, about 2 by 1 inches
2 cloves garlic
Juice from 1 large lemon, about 3 Tbsp
2 Tbsp grated Parmesan or Romano cheese
½ tsp sea salt
About 6 grinds black pepper

DIRECTIONS

Put all ingredients in a high-speed blender and blend on high for 1 to 2 minutes or until well combined. Chill for 1 to 2 hours before serving.

BASIC BROWN GRAVY

PREP TIME **5 MINUTES**
COOK TIME **15 MINUTES**
YIELD **4–6 SERVINGS**

No meat-heavy feast like Season 5's vegan debacle is complete without this classic condiment, so why not whip up a batch from scratch?

INGREDIENTS

2 Tbsp butter
2 Tbsp all-purpose flour
2 cups beef broth or stock
2 Tbsp tomato paste
2 teaspoons grainy Dijon mustard, such as Grey Poupon

2 Tbsp Worcestershire sauce
2 tsp fish sauce, such as Red Boat
Freshly cracked black pepper

DIRECTIONS

Melt butter in a large skillet over low heat then whisk in remaining ingredients. Let simmer on low for 5 minutes.

CREAMY HORSERADISH SAUCE

PREP TIME 15 MINUTES
CHILL TIME 1–2 HOURS
YIELD 16 SERVINGS

When cattlemen celebrate a successful season or sale, there's only one way to celebrate: steak. Serve this sauce alongside your would-be rancher's rib-eye and watch them light up.

INGREDIENTS

- ⅔ cup sour cream
- ½ cup mayonnaise
- 2–3 Tbsp horseradish
- ¼ cup white vinegar
- 1 Tbsp chives
- ¼ tsp salt
- ¼ tsp pepper
- 1 tsp Worcestershire sauce
- 1 tsp granulated white sugar

DIRECTIONS

Put all ingredients in a high-speed blender and blend on high for 1 to 2 minutes or until well combined. Chill for 1 to 2 hours before serving.

STEAK SAUCE

PREP TIME 15 MINUTES
CHILL TIME 1–2 HOURS
YIELD 16 SERVINGS

Gator wouldn't give up his secret recipe, but this kicked-up steak sauce is surely worthy of any table, Dutton or otherwise.

INGREDIENTS

- 1 cup raisins
- 1 medium orange, about 5 oz, peeled
- Juice from 2 medium lemons, about ¼ cup
- ½ cup tomato puree
- 1 Tbsp tomato paste
- 1 clove garlic
- ¼ cup malt vinegar
- ½ cup white vinegar
- ½ tsp celery salt
- 1 tsp onion flakes
- 1 Tbsp fish sauce, such as Red Boat
- ½ tsp liquid smoke
- 1 Tbsp Dijon mustard
- ½ tsp kosher salt
- ½ tsp ground black pepper

DIRECTIONS

Put all ingredients in a high-speed blender and blend on high for 1 to 2 minutes or until well combined. Chill for 1 to 2 hours before serving.

PEPPERED WHITE GRAVY

PREP TIME 15 MINUTES
YIELD 16 SERVINGS

Your biscuits and gravy will be almost as good as Gator's if you take the time to make your own white gravy.

INGREDIENTS

- 3 Tbsp butter or bacon grease
- 3 Tbsp all-purpose flour
- 1 cup vegetable broth or stock
- 1 cup half-and-half
- ½ tsp onion flakes
- ½ tsp garlic powder
- ½ tsp ground black pepper
- ½ tsp red chili powder, hot or mild
- ½ tsp liquid smoke
- Salt to taste
- 4 sausage patties (elk, beef, soy, pork, etc.), cooked and crumbled, optional
- Smoked paprika for serving

DIRECTIONS

Melt the butter or bacon grease in a medium saucepan over medium-low. Whisk in the flour to make a paste. Gradually whisk in the broth and half-and-half until smooth, then reduce the heat to warm and stir in the onion flakes, garlic powder, black pepper, chili powder, liquid smoke and salt to taste. Add sausage if using and garnish with smoked paprika.

HABANERO MUSTARD

PREP TIME 15 MINUTES
CHILL TIME 1–2 HOURS
YIELD 16 SERVINGS

When your guests are as fiery as Rip on a bad day, match their intensity with this kickin' condiment.

INGREDIENTS

- 2 Tbsp yellow mustard
- ¼ cup tahini
- 1 (2-oz) slice white onion
- 1 habanero chile, destemmed
- 1 medium seedless orange, peeled, about 5–6 oz
- 2 cloves garlic
- Juice from 1 medium lemon, about 2 Tbsp
- ¼ cup white vinegar
- 1 tsp ground turmeric
- 1 tsp dry mustard
- ½ tsp salt
- ½ tsp granulated cane sugar

DIRECTIONS

Put all ingredients in a high-speed blender and blend on high for 1 to 2 minutes or until well combined. Chill for 1 to 2 hours before serving.

TIPS FROM THE TRAIL

If you're not quite ready for the bite of a habanero pepper, try something with less intensity, like cayenne.

A man crosses a Montana stream with his horse. Many of *Yellowstone*'s stunt riders are decorated rodeo champions champion such as Andrea Fappani.

Maggie Dutton's Old- Fashioned Blackberry and Buttermilk Cobbler, pg. 180.

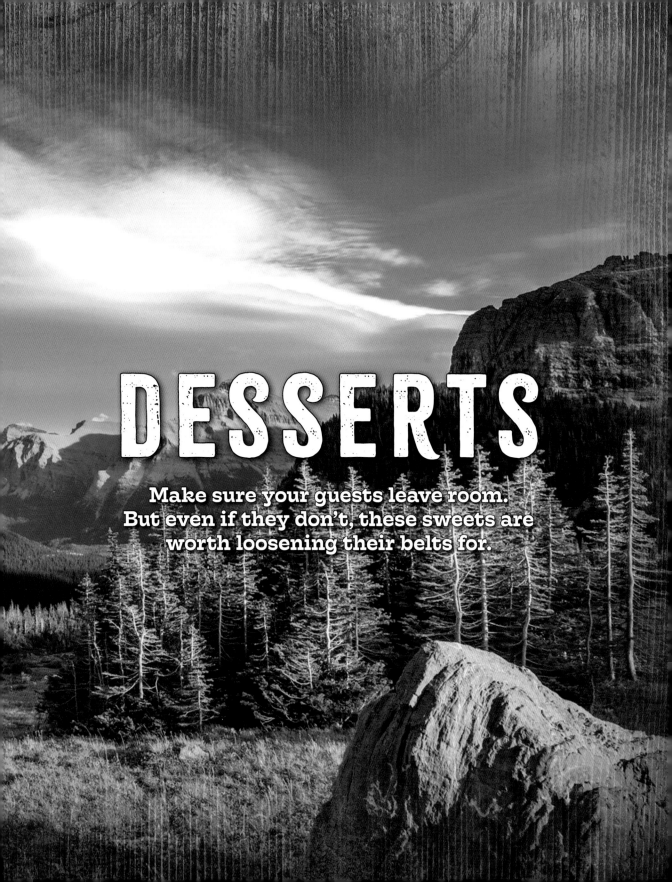

DESSERTS

Make sure your guests leave room.
But even if they don't, these sweets are
worth loosening their belts for.

Big Chocolate Chip and Sea Salt Cookies

YOUNG JOHN DUTTON MIGHT HAVE THOUGHT HE WAS SLICK TAKING A COOKIE FROM THE JAR EVERY NIGHT, BUT HIS DAD KNEW THE WHOLE TIME. WHO CAN BLAME A KID WHEN THE COOKIES ARE THIS GOOD?

PREP TIME 15 MINUTES
COOK TIME 15 MINUTES
YIELD 12–15 SERVINGS

INGREDIENTS

2¼ cups all-purpose flour
½ tsp baking soda
½ tsp baking powder
1 Tbsp cornstarch
½ tsp fine sea salt
1 cup butter
1 cup light brown sugar
½ cup granulated cane sugar
2 eggs
1 Tbsp pure vanilla extract
2 cups chocolate chips or chunks
1–2 Tbsp flaky sea salt, such as Maldon, for sprinkling

DIRECTIONS

1. Preheat the oven to 350 degrees F. Line 2 18-by-13-inch rimmed half-sheet baking pans with parchment paper or baking mats.
2. In a bowl, whisk together the flour, baking soda, baking powder, cornstarch and fine sea salt. Set aside.
3. In another bowl, combine the butter, sugars, eggs and vanilla. Mix in the dry ingredients, then fold in the chocolate.
4. Spoon 3 Tbsp-sized scoops of dough onto the baking sheets, leaving 2 inches around each.
5. Bake for 12 to 15 minutes or until golden brown. Sprinkle with flaky sea salt as soon as the cookies come out of the oven.

TIPS FROM THE TRAIL

Maldon Smoked Sea Salt is especially good on these. Chocolate chips come in varying degrees of sweetness. Use the variety you like best.

Maple Pecan Pie

APPLE PIE MIGHT GET ALL THE ATTENTION, BUT FOR US, THERE'S NOTHING MORE AMERICAN THAN THIS PECAN PIE, WITH AN EXTRA NOD TO OUR MIGHTY FORESTS THANKS TO MAPLE SYRUP.

PREP TIME 20 MINUTES
COOK TIME 1 HOUR
YIELD 8 SERVINGS

INGREDIENTS

- 2 cups pecan halves
- 2 sheets refrigerated pie crust, room temperature
- 3 large eggs, lightly beaten
- ½ cup light or dark brown sugar
- 1 cup pure maple syrup
- 3 Tbsp melted butter
- 1 Tbsp pure vanilla extract
- ½ tsp salt

SPECIAL EQUIPMENT

1 (3-to-4-inch) maple leaf cookie cutter

DIRECTIONS

1. Preheat the oven to 350 degrees F.
2. Toast pecans in a single layer on a baking sheet until browned, about 5 to 8 minutes.
3. Line a 9-inch pie pan with one sheet of crust. Pierce the bottom of the dough with a fork, then crimp the top edge.
4. Gently whisk together the eggs, sugar, maple syrup, melted butter, vanilla and salt, then stir in the toasted pecans. Spoon filling into the pan.
5. Unroll the other crust and cut out a maple leaf. Refrigerate the leaf for 15 minutes before placing on top of the pie.
6. Bake at 350 degrees F for 20 minutes, then cover the pie with aluminum foil and cook for 35 to 40 minutes longer or until set. Let cool for 1 hour before serving.

TIPS FROM THE TRAIL

If you want to make your pecan pie look even fancier, finish it off with a light dusting of powdered sugar.

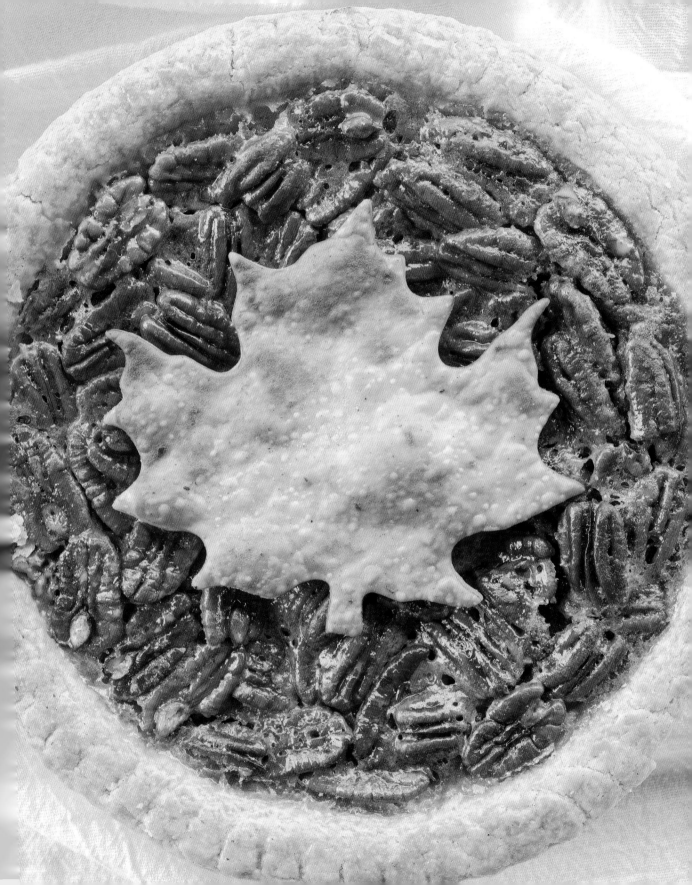

Triple Chocolate Flourless Cake With Fudge Frosting

AS JOHN DUTTON TELLS CARTER IN SEASON 4, SOMETIMES IT'S OK TO HAVE CAKE WITH YOUR STEAK, AS OPPOSED TO AFTER.

PREP TIME 15 MINUTES
COOK TIME 25 MINUTES
YIELD 8 SERVINGS

INGREDIENTS

- 1 cup chocolate chips
- 1 stick (½ cup) butter, plus more for greasing the pan
- ¾ cup granulated cane sugar
- ¼ tsp salt
- 1 tsp ground cinnamon
- 1 tsp pure vanilla extract
- 3 large eggs, lightly beaten
- ½ cup unsweetened Dutch process cocoa powder, such as King Arthur's Burgundy Cocoa

FUDGE FROSTING

- 1 cup chocolate chips
- 2 Tbsp heavy cream
- 1 cup butter, room temperature
- 3 cups confectioners' sugar, sifted

DIRECTIONS

1. Preheat the oven to 375 degrees F.
2. Grease a 10-inch cast iron skillet.
3. Put 1 cup chocolate chips along with the butter in a microwave-safe mixing bowl. Heat on 50 percent power until butter is melted and chips are soft, about 1 minute. Stir with a butter knife until chips melt.
4. Stir in the sugar, salt, cinnamon, vanilla and eggs. Add cocoa powder and mix to combine.
5. Transfer the batter to the skillet and bake for 25 minutes. The top should have a thin crust. Remove from oven and let cool.
6. While the cake is cooling, prepare the frosting. Add chocolate chips and cream to a microwave-safe mixing bowl and heat on 50 percent power until the chips are soft, about 1 minute.
7. Beat the butter with an electric mixer on low until light and creamy, about 2 minutes. Add the confectioners' sugar a ½ cup at a time, beating to incorporate after each addition, then pour in the chocolate mixture and beat until light and fluffy, about 3 minutes more.
8. Frost the cooled cake and serve with a big spoon.

Maggie Dutton's Old-Fashioned Blackberry and Buttermilk Cobbler

PIE'S LESS FRILLY BUT JUST AS DELICIOUS COUSIN, COBBLER IS A CLASSIC DESSERT THAT'S PRACTICALLY MADE FOR YOUR FAMILY'S HEIRLOOM CAST IRON CASSEROLE PAN.

PREP TIME 15 MINUTES
COOK TIME 30 MINUTES
YIELD 8 SERVINGS

INGREDIENTS

- 36 oz blackberries, defrosted if frozen
- ¼ cup granulated sugar, divided
- ½ tsp kosher salt
- Juice from 1 medium lemon, about 2–3 Tbsp
- 2 Tbsp Canadian whiskey, such as Black Label
- 2 tsp arrowroot powder
- 8 raw 1½-inch buttermilk biscuits, see pg. 165

DIRECTIONS

1. Preheat the oven to 350 degrees F.
2. Toss the berries with 3 Tbsp of the sugar, salt, lemon juice, whiskey and arrowroot powder. Transfer to a 9-by-13-inch or 3-quart casserole dish. Lay the raw biscuits on top, then dust with the remaining 1 Tbsp sugar.
3. Bake for 25 to 30 minutes or until the biscuits are browned and cooked through and the berries are syrupy and bubbling. Let cool for 5 minutes before serving.

DID YOU KNOW?

According to *The Oxford Companion to Food*, cobbler has been a staple in the U.S. since the 1850s, making it an authentic part of the pioneer experience.

Montana Flathead Cherry Galette

MAKE USE OF SOME OF *YELLOWSTONE*'S HOME STATE'S MOST TASTIEST STONE FRUITS WITH THIS DELICIOUS DESSERT.

PREP TIME 30 MINUTES
WAIT TIME 30 MINUTES
COOK TIME 50 MINUTES
YIELD 8–10 SERVINGS

INGREDIENTS

- 4 cups sifted all-purpose flour
- 1 Tbsp sugar
- 1 tsp salt
- 1½ cups cold butter, cut into ¼-inch cubes
- 1 large egg, lightly beaten
- 1 tsp white vinegar
- ½ cup cold water
- 2 cups pitted cherries, thawed and drained if frozen
- ½ tsp arrowroot powder
- 1 Tbsp granulated cane sugar
- 1 Tbsp lemon juice
- ½ tsp cinnamon
- 1 cup fresh cherries with pits and stems, recommended
- Confectioners' sugar for dusting

DIRECTIONS

1. Whisk together the flour, sugar and salt. Add the cold butter, then squish and pinch the butter pieces into the flour.

2. In a separate bowl, whisk together the egg, vinegar and water.

3. Pour the egg mixture over the flour mixture and mix until the dough comes together.

4. Divide into 2 balls. Wrap each in plastic wrap. Refrigerate one of them for 30 minutes. Freeze the other for another use, such as pasties or pecan pie dough (pg. 176).

5. Preheat the oven to 400 degrees F.

6. Place the pitted cherries in a bowl. Toss with the arrowroot powder, cane sugar, lemon juice and cinnamon.

7. Remove the dough from the refrigerator and roughly roll out onto a nonstick baking mat or large piece of parchment paper to a ¼-inch thickness. Transfer the mat or parchment with the dough to a half-sheet baking pan. Place the cherry mixture in the center, leaving a 2-inch border of crust surrounding it.

8. Fold the exposed crust over the top of the cherries, leaving a large area of uncovered fruit in the middle. Bake until the crust is golden, about 40 to 45 minutes.

9. Remove and let cool, then nestle the fresh cherries among the cooked cherries with their stems facing up, if desired. Dust the crust with confectioners' sugar and slice with a pizza cutter.

Campfire-Style Cornbread Pudding

A CLASSIC DESSERT GETS A MAKEOVER WORTHY OF A YELLOWSTONE COWBOY THANKS TO DOWN-HOME CORNBREAD.

PREP TIME 30 MINUTES
COOK TIME 50 MINUTES
YIELD 8–10 SERVINGS

INGREDIENTS

- 1 prepared cornbread (see pg. 57), cut into 1-to-2-inch chunks
- ½ cup melted butter
- ½ cup sugar
- 1 cup grated Parmesan, divided
- 2 cups half-and-half
- 2 Tbsp vanilla extract
- 1½ tsp salt
- 6 large eggs
- Honey, for serving

DIRECTIONS

1. Preheat the oven to 350 degrees F.
2. Place the cornbread chunks into either 4 prepared cast iron ramekins or a 9-by-13-inch baking dish.
3. Combine the melted butter, sugar, half the Parmesan, half-and-half, vanilla and salt in a large mixing bowl, then whisk in the eggs until well combined. Pour over the cornbread and let sit for 10 minutes. Cover and bake for 30 minutes, then uncover, sprinkle on remaining Parmesan and bake for 20 minutes more or until browned and set.
4. Let cool for 5 minutes. Drizzle with honey.

TIPS FROM THE TRAIL

If you're really pinched for time, you can use premade cornbread, but we find the best results come from a fresh-baked pan.

INDEX

CONVERSION GUIDE

VOLUME

¼ tsp	1 mL
½ tsp	2 mL
1 tsp	5 mL
1 Tbsp	15 mL
¼ cup	50mL
⅓ cup	75 mL
½ cup	125 mL
⅔ cup	150 mL
¾ cup	175 mL
1 cup	250 mL
1 quart	1 liter
1½ quarts	1.5 liters
2 quarts	2 liters
2½ quarts	2.5 liters
3 quarts	3 liters
4 quarts	4 liters

TEMPERATURE

32° F	0° C
212° F	100° C
250° F	120° C
275° F	140° C
300° F	150° C
325° F	160° C
350° F	180° C
375° F	190° C
400° F	200° C
425° F	220° C
450° F	230° C
475° F	240° C
500° F	260° C

LENGTH

⅛ in	3 mm
¼ in	6 mm
½ in	13 mm
¾ in	19 mm
1 in	2.5 cm
2 in	5 cm

WEIGHT

1 oz	30 g
2 oz	55 g
3 oz	85 g
4 oz / ¼ lb	115 g
8 oz / ½ lb	225 g
16 oz / 1 lb	455 g
32 oz / 2 lb	910 g

AUTHOR PHOTO: JASON WILLIS

JACKIE ALPERS is an award-winning cookbook author, food photographer and recipe developer who experiments with regional culinary influences while exploring food history and culture and the relationship people have with food and drink. She teaches creativity in the kitchen from her home in Tucson, Arizona.

Media Lab Books
For inquiries, call 646-449-8614

Copyright © 2023 Jackie Alpers

Published by Topix Media Lab
14 Wall Street, Suite 3C
New York, NY 10005

Printed in China

ISBN-13: 978-1-956403-20-6
ISBN-10: 1-956403-20-5

CEO Tony Romando

Vice President & Publisher Phil Sexton
Senior Vice President of Sales & New Markets Tom Mifsud
Vice President of Retail Sales & Logistics Linda Greenblatt
Chief Financial Officer Vandana Patel
Manufacturing Director Nancy Puskuldjian
Digital Marketing & Strategy Manager Elyse Gregov

Chief Content Officer Jeff Ashworth
Director of Editorial Operations Courtney Kerrigan
Senior Acquisitions Editor Noreen Henson
Creative Director Susan Dazzo
Photo Director Dave Weiss
Managing Editor Tara Sherman

Content Editor Tim Baker
Content Designer Alyssa Bredin Quirós
Features Editor Trevor Courneen
Associate Editor Juliana Sharaf
Designers Glen Karpowich, Mikio Sakai
Copy Editor & Fact Checker Madeline Raynor
Assistant Photo Editor Jenna Addesso

ALL RECIPE PHOTOS: Jackie Alpers

COVER: Cowboy: Nancy Greifenhagen Western Photography/Alamy. Prairie: Sylvain Didier/Alamy. Shed: Jake Elko/Stocksy
BACK COVER: PER Images/Stocksy

PHOTOS: 2 Epicurean/iStock; 5 From top: Shutterstock; Nikita Sursin/Stocksy; Shutterstock; 6 Shutterstock; 7 Shutterstock (2); 8 EMPPhotography/iStock; 10 Shutterstock; 44 Ed Freeman/Stone/Getty Images; 46 Shutterstock; 70 Boogich/iStock; 72 Shutterstock; 73 From top: Cameron Whitman/Socksy; Shutterstock; 74 Shutterstock; 75 Shutterstock; 76 Taha Raja/500px/Getty Images; 78 Shutterstock; 110 Viktor Vichev/EyeEm/Getty Images; 112 Shutterstock; 116 Chase Dekker Wild-Life Images/Moment/Getty Images; 118 Shutterstock; 132 Chase Dekker Wild-Life Images/Moment/Getty Images; 134 Shutterstock; 168 Epicurean/iStock; 172 Shutterstock. All other photos: Shutterstock

Indexing by R studio T, NYC